THE TEMPLATE

A Holonomic Model
of Transcendence

Juliet and Jiva Carter

SOWELU PUBLISHING

The Template-A Holonomic Model of Transcendence
Copyright © 2005 Juliet Carter and Jiva Carter
All rights reserved.
First printing, May 2005
Second printing (revised), June 2006

Printing History: printed under previous name, **The Template Workbook 1 Level 1**
in the United Kingdom, October 2004

Published by: Sowelu Publishing
400 West Third St. Ste. D100
Santa Rosa, CA 95401

Printed and bound in the United States of America and the United Kingdom.

ISBN 0-9722753-0-4

Editors: Nick Marchmont, Jennifer Carmen
Cover design, geometry photographs: Jiva Carter
Layout: Jiva Carter, Teresa Jalon

Our thanks to

Cosmos, Jennifer, Margo,
Tantra, Teresa

Editors
Jennifer, Nick

Ambassador Support UK
Cosmos, Claudie, Jennifer
Jeremy, Lynn, Nick, Rhian

Ambassador Support USA
Margo, Shahida, Tantra

Special thanks to

Suzy

and

the major - domo

The Template Model

The Workbook

This Template Workbook is a companion manual for the first
3 Ceremony workshops. However, it also serves as a comprehensive body
of information to guide you through these challenging times
of personal and planetary transformation.

From the healing of the fundamental Human condition to the realignment
of the cosmogenic order of our solar system, The Template model
is a holonomic whole system that reveals the dynamics of transcendence
in intelligent and digestible terms, as it bridges the geometric signal of light,
the circuitry of the endocrine system, DNA activation
and the morphogenetic field.

The fundamental requisite in this journey of transcendence is the reconnection
of circuitry that leads to the resurrection of the original and complete
genetic code embedded in the Human matrix. The essential experience
of reconnection requires interface with the alchemical components
present within The Template Ceremonies. The transformational codes
are not included in this book as these alchemical components
cannot be contained and experienced via the written word -
they must be transmitted and received Human to Human
within the arena of Sacred Ceremony.

**To attend a Template Ceremony
please contact a Template Ambassador.**

www.originalinnocence.com
www.thetemplate.org

TABLE OF CONTENTS

PHASE I

FOUNDATION

The Ceremony of Original Innocence

PHASE II

ACTIVATION AND INTEGRATION
The 13th Circuit Ceremony

PHASE II

ACTIVATION AND INTEGRATION
The Sacred Breath Ceremony

The Template Series of Ceremonies
A Holonomic Model of Transcendence

There are 6 Ceremonies in The Template. Each Ceremony is a fractal within the holonomic model of transcendence.

The Template itself is an interactive schematic that provides a whole system through which the resurrection of the original Human blueprint is achieved, via the reconnection of bio-circuitry, through coded Ceremony. Each Ceremony reconnects a series of circuits within the Human bio-computer. Each series of circuits creates a layer of reinstated electromagnetic integrity that in turn interacts with the circuits reconnected in all the other Ceremonies... it is a holonomic system.

This system is divided into 3 phases:

Foundation

*The Ceremony of Original Innocence
- the reconnection of the basal 12 Circuits.*

Activation and Integration

*The 13th Circuit Ceremony
- the reconnection of the 13th Circuit.*

*The Sacred Breath Ceremony
- the reconnection of the 7 Pranic Circuits.*

Actualization

*The Source Ceremony
- the reconnection of the 5 Source Circuits.*

*The Temple of Time Ceremony
- the reconnection of the 7 Circuits of Time,
synthesizing the co-ordinates of time and space
into the incarnate body presence.*

*The Ceremony of Galactic Unity
- the reconnection of the 'One' Circuit.*

Your Workbook

*This book has been designed as a companion manual
for the first 3 Ceremony workshops in The Template series:*

The Ceremony of Original Innocence

The 13th Circuit Ceremony

The Sacred Breath Ceremony

*The first 7 chapters of the book outline the governing
systems of the higher physics of creation that form the matrix
of The Template as a whole system. Your chosen Ambassador
will be fluent in the understanding of this system.*

*The section of the manual that begins the 2nd phase
of The Template (Activation and Integration) introduces
Sacred Geometry as an alchemical component within
The 13th Circuit Ceremony and The Sacred Breath Ceremony.*

*It also deals with the geometric Soul Covenant,
the pranic causeway/mechanism and Sacred Breath.
Your Ambassador will guide you through the information
relevant to the Ceremony you are to experience on that day.*

*This book covers subjects pertaining to the higher physics
of creation that are the foundation of The Template system
- the science of transcendence. The essence of each subject
has been documented in a brief and simple form
as is appropriate for a workbook.*

*The Template schematic has been downloaded through
the collaboration of the authors and a Consciousness
that can be described as the Planetary Evolutionary Guides,
also referred to as 'The Bird Tribe'.*

The Template is a working, interactive schematic that initiates transformation through the reconnection of the life-giving energy system of circuitry that animates the Human entity on every level. The reintroduction of electromagnetic dataflow, via the delivery system of circuitry, allows us to translate and utilize the full spectrum of life-force emanating from the Source of Creation - a creation code that activates and rejuvenates the Human heart/body/mind system, resurrecting the dormant genetic material in the DNA.

The impact of circuitry reconnection involves the many visible and invisible interactive, co-creative energy systems that comprise the Human hologram. The energy is delivered by the circuitry in its primal form, to be translated and utilized by the chakra system, the endocrine system, the pranic mechanism and the Soul Covenant embedded in the Human matrix. This acceleration of integrated and synthesized Source Intelligence, translated through the Human bio-computational awareness, affects the individual/mass consciousness frequency, transforming the morphogenetic field and constructing a new paradigm of consensus reality. This is the 'science of transcendence' that is intrinsic to The Template model and is covered in this book.

The Template model is a new paradigm schematic and as such, the language downloaded in the process of outlining its design holds the frequency of an expanded immortal harmonic. It is the sacred responsibility of the visionary to receive and deliver information without censorship.

At times, the information is received in states of extreme receptivity and the comprehension of the writer is suspended in order to maintain the purity of this information without diluting it to suit personal limitations.

To downgrade this information into mundane language is to lose a vital harmonic, for the language itself is transformational. When physics reaches a certain depth, it synthesizes with the divine Tantric potencies of creation and becomes poetry. As with poetry it must be understood with the heart and the body as well as the mind.

*Open yourself to this information and enter into meditation with it,
allowing it to dissolve your judgment and preconceptions.
Tune in to how it makes you feel.
If there are portions of the book that you do not at first understand,
put it aside, wait a while and try again.
Like any new language, it becomes comprehensible through
the speaking of it... read it aloud, preferably to another person.*

*There are concepts outlined here, such as immortality,
that go against the tides of what you have been deeply programmed
to believe. Have patience with yourself and allow the time and space
for these concepts to germinate and blossom within you.
As you reconnect more circuits, you will be better able to comprehend
the information and you will develop your own innate understanding
as the knowledge awakens within you.*

*There are pages in this book upon which there is only one statement
with a geometric background. These are 'mantras of creation',
opening portals into the new paradigm continuum.
The geometric forms alchemically assist assimilation
and integration of this information, not through reprogramming,
but through resonance. Meditate on these sound bites,
make copies and post them around your home
and you will find that they will affect not only
what you think but also **how** you think.*

*The Template model is not an intellectual/philosophical exercise
but a way of being and seeing, seeing the almost forgotten concepts
of sentient sovereignty, of true Human freedom as a reality.*

The Healing Process

*The structure of The Template may appear to be somewhat
scientific, resting as it does upon the higher physics of creation.
However, the impact of the transformation is emotional, physical
and mental, translating immediately into life experience.
The circuitry reconnection deals with forgiveness,
addiction, fear, guilt, shame, anger and grief...
all the pain of being Human.*

*When your leg has fallen asleep, before it 'wakes up', there is
a period of pins and needles - a transitional phase of discomfort.
Any dynamic transformational process is going to bring with it
a degree of discomfort. Be aware that discomfort is a good thing
and a very real indication of transformation. Know that The Template
process of transformation is an impeccable system, organically
regulated by each initiate's ability to embrace change on every level.
This process takes into consideration the individual's innate
nature and their present domestic situation.
It is a totally safe system.*

**To embrace forgiveness is to embody the living mandala of love
upon which is based the fundamental Human ethic.**

*The initiate needs to be aware that the core necessity of forgiveness
is the fundamental basis for spiritual advancement
and primary healing. As the saying goes, 'You will not go to the stars
angry at your mother!' There are specific circuits that will
support the forgiving process.*

*Ultimately, it is the reintroduction of circuitry, the synthesis
of Source Intelligence, the redefinition of that Source in the Human
psyche and the embodiment of that core spiritual identity
that will bring sustainable healing and peace.
Your Ambassador will suggest that you regroup in order to share
your transformational experiences, to study the information
and help each other through resonance. Whenever possible
the Ambassador will lead these gatherings.*

*As Einstein said, "The problems we have cannot be solved
at the same level of thinking with which we created them."
The Ceremonies are a solution that exists outside of the problem,
a new paradigm healing that takes into consideration
our genetically modified DNA and our intrinsic immortal nature.
This knowledge changes the way in which we see ourselves,
our world and our reality and, thus, our modes of healing.
Particularly relevant is the concept of healing at the fulcrum level
- changing the pattern of behavior, not by attempting to alter
the manifestation of that behavior but by affecting
the fountainhead from which it emerges.*

*Many of you will find that the healers you have been going to will
register a change in your energy field created by the acceleration
of electromagnetic input, due to the reconnected circuitry
(explained further in this book). It may assist your practitioner
to know some details of the work you have experienced.
However, be aware that it is not uncommon for those who
do not understand a process to judge it out-of-hand.
You may find that it is your practitioners who will notice
your changes as they are trained to read energy.
Other people may simply be drawn to your lighter vibration.*

*We have found that the most useful after-Ceremony care can
be achieved through simple non-verbal therapies such as
bodywork and water therapies. These modalities function
energetically, and therefore can allow the integration
of new energies without intellectual interference.
Should you feel the necessity for counseling, be aware that
a counselor who has experienced The Template Ceremonies
will be far better equipped to assist you.
There are some Ambassadors who are also counselors
and as this work gains more and more exposure
the number of these Ambassadors will increase.
Although your Ambassador may not have any clinical training
as a counselor, he or she will have total understanding
of the mechanics of Ceremonial healing and the consequences
of reconnecting circuitry. This will greatly assist you
with your integration process.*

Tools only work when you use them!

Although the very action of a reconnection creates immediate change to a degree, your conscious participation is required to integrate and synthesize the optimum transformational impact of reconnected circuitry. There are certain tools to assist integration and to trigger acceleration, such as vegetarianism and conscious breathing. These tools are explored in this book .

Towards the back of the book is The Sacred Day Ceremony that has been specifically given to assist the initiate to stay grounded in the flow of the new frequencies. This is an incredibly powerful Ceremony that holds the frequency signature of the entire Template.

This book will explain The Template to the best of our ability at this time. However, as more Source Intelligence distils within the crucible of our comprehension, we will expand upon the information in further publications.

Workbook II will deal with the 4th and 5th Ceremonies in the Actualization phase. Check the website to know when it becomes available.

We at the Center for Transcendent Ceremony welcome you to The Template circle of transformation.

We hope you enjoy your flight!

*The energetic nature
of consciousness
that fosters all life
is integrated by the Human
heart/body/mind/soul
via the bio-circuitry*

The Journey

*As you embark upon the Foundation Ceremony,
you are embarking upon a journey of healing, forgiveness,
remembrance, resurrection and, ultimately, transcendence
of the dualistic, fear-based mortal paradigm.*

*The Template is not just a series of workshops; it is a chosen way
of being, a life path. To choose this path is to embrace the Human
as a magnificent masterpiece of immortal design, capable
of transcending the limitations of duality and able to access
any time or energy level in the universe.*

*Reaching beyond the superficiality of a feel-good system designed
to make this fear-based reality work for you, The Template reaches
to the far horizons of Humanity's divine potential - the potential
that lies within the Soul Covenant.*

*This journey is one of liberation and empowerment that takes us into
the ancient history of Humanity's true origins to retrieve our soul's
lineage and our celestial seeding; a history that defies the notions
of original sin, shame and guilt that have shaped the foundations
of the orthodox religions which continue to tear the world apart.
This is a journey of self-discovery, unfolding from within
as the story is told from the weave of our own genetic fabric,
stored within the labyrinths of the cerebral cortex...
the 'Temple of Remembrance'.*

*The Template is dedicated to the recovery of this ancestral
remembrance, the original innocence of our divine nature,
the resurrection of the transcendental Human.*

*That which is now being translated in the media as a global
crisis is, in fact, the deterioration of the material field.
This deterioration is the darkness of the womb that gives
birth to a new model of existence, a new paradigm.
As circuitry is reconnected, the resurgence of divine life-force
re-establishes our true identities beyond the psychosocial, chemical,
electromagnetic and religious manipulation of consciousness.*

Our spiritual identity is energetically redefined and stabilized through electromagnetic reconnection to Source; fear is diminished and replaced by the real courage that comes from knowing that there is no death, no separation...nothing can be lost, for we are the invincible radiance of eternal life.

As we approach the completion of this cycle, the stars and planets move in and out of the grand crosses and alignments that are bringing the momentum of this age to its grand finale. The Human race, its mother planet and the entire solar system, are in the throes of an evolutionary acceleration. The full promise of conscious evolution that is offered through the symbiosis of our relationship with the solar system has been hugely undermined by the magnetic interference of a celestial body that is not a part of the symbiotic alchemy stipulated in the coding of the original Human blueprint; a situation that has impacted the vital functions of Human neurobiology and atrophied the endocrine system. This interference will be overridden by the magnetic counterbalance of a critical mass of fully resurrected Human units of circuitry and the re-instigation of the true space/time co-ordinates dictated by the Sun and the original solar system.

Embedded in the Human matrix is the Soul Covenant that holds the harmonic of our symbiotic relationship with the evolution of our mother planet, the solar system and the galactic cosmology. It is the primary function of The Template model to resurrect this Covenant and reunify its immortal harmonic with the physical Human expression as it was originally designed, prior to our genetic modification.

This journey of resurrection will bring initiates to a place in which they will begin to take stock of their lifestyle and to clearly evaluate the global situation without denial. The reconnection of specific circuitry will assist initiates in taking a courageous overview of the Human condition - circuitry that re-establishes conscious awareness of the quintessential Human identity by returning the electromagnetic integrity of the soul's ancestral lineage and its celestial seeding. This assists initiates to make choices based on a new and empowered point of reference, helping them to recognize their attachments to limitation, making way for a new model of existence that redefines consciousness, and their connection to Source, as their most valuable commodity.

*"I recommend their work (Ceremonies of The Template) as a key
to what we all need to be doing right now as 2012 approaches."*

John Major Jenkins: author of 'Maya Cosmogenesis 2012'

*As the stargate of 2012 approaches, the celestial alignment is opening
a portal of opportunity of a magnitude never before experienced
on this planet. A massive influx of radiant intelligence infuses
the crystalline chambers of our Sun to be translated upon every ray
of light transmitted to Earth. The reconnection of circuitry, instigated
by the alchemical ceremonies of The Template, will enable you
to embrace and prepare for this journey of transcendence
by resurrecting the Human ability to translate the full spectrum
of light - for light is the language of transcendence.*

*To assist the integration and synthesis of the Source Intelligence
delivered by the reconnection of circuitry so that it becomes
a fully conscious part of your incarnate presence, we advise
that you study the information laid out in this workbook.*

*The symbiotic relationship between the number of reconnected units
of circuitry and the morphogenetic field of global consciousness
will also dictate the degree of individual acceleration.
This is explored in the next chapter, The Science of Transcendence.*

*Circuitry draws
the heart/body/mind
system into the nurture
of the holonomic
life-giving mechanism
that brings in the
Benevolent Heart
of Creation*

The Science of Transcendence
Circuitry, the Endocrine System and DNA

*As we witness the acceleration of deterioration within the social,
political and economic world structures, it is beneficial
to understand the evolutionary influences that are driving this age.
By so doing we can consciously implicate ourselves within
the phenomenal opportunity for transmutation that is available
during this phase of culmination. It is the transitional phase
of conception and deterioration in any cycle which creates
the powerful frictions that open the portals for transcendence.
It is during the degenerative phase that the rotting fruit
falls away and the new seed is expelled.
When you consider the underlying premises of these structures
that define our present mundane existence it is no wonder
that they are collapsing!*

**This global crisis is not a dark event but a redistribution
of natural power created by an immense influx of light.**

*This influx is being created by the maturing influences of a solar
system that is itself reaching higher and higher states of cosmic
comprehension, transmitting to Earth and its inhabitants
ever new spectrums of radiance data - light.
Massive beams of this 'hyper-creation code' are emanating
from the galactic core to sweep their influence through the solar
system, activating and integrating the symbiotic evolutionary
covenants that lie dormant and waiting in every cell of every
living creation - for this kiss of light to awaken them
to a new model of existence, a new paradigm.*

*It will be the degree to which we are able to translate and utilize
this light code that will allow us to break the barriers of illusion
set by this dualistic paradigm and the genetic modifications
that are in resonance with it.*

It is because of this light influx that we are now able to answer
the three most fundamental questions that define us
as conscious Human entities:

" Who am I? Where am I from? Why am I here?"

In order to do so, however, we must have some ability
to understand the implicate order of our own creation and, to some
degree, the mechanical complexity of the reality in which we find
ourselves. No living thing within creation exists in isolation.
The interconnected, interactive, co-creative individual system
of each entity is a fractal of the one holographic system
that encompasses the subatomic to the multi-universal.

The Template model of transcendence encompasses a design
and progression that is in total resonance with the vibratory
infrastructure of the primal creation code, a mirror frequency
that duplicates the synchronomic systems that govern all
of existence, honoring the Human as a fractal component,
in symbiotic resonance with not only its mother bio-system,
the Earth, but also the solar/galactic/universal holography.

The Template of transcendence links alchemical
Ceremony with brain chemistry, circuitry, the endocrine system,
neurobiology, DNA, the archetypal arena and the morphogenetic
field to reveal the holonomic system of creation
that births and binds the Human hologram.

Historically, we have left the mechanics of creation to the scientists,
our sense of justice to the lawyers and judges, the integrity
of our social structures to the governments, and our spiritual
identities to the priests who act as mediators between ourselves
and the Benevolence of our Creation. These 'experts'
have wrapped these concepts in their own language
and removed them from the grasp of our sensibilities.
The allocation of our most fundamental power-base has caused
the atrophy of our own decision-making abilities.

It is time to take back our power.

*Through alternative healing methods we have become aware of our
electromagnetic energy fields and the importance of our neurobiology
and biochemistry. Through this, and the discoveries made in the field
of genetics, we are becoming aware that there is a science
to spirituality and that our chemistry affects our consciousness.
Taking this further, we are now making the connection between
the mutant state of our DNA and the present global insanities
of war, genocide and endless Human suffering.*

*Humanity is awakening to a new body-awareness as we are driven
to gain mastery over our own inner workings and to discover how we
interact with and co-create the reality in which we find ourselves.
Instead of searching for the out-of-body experience in order to realize
our spiritual identity, we are beginning to understand that our
physical being is the manifestation of that identity, realizing
that the physical vehicles we embody will allow us to transcend
this fear-based reality and create, through the resurrection
of our full genetic Human potential, a new paradigm, a golden age.*

This is the science of transcendence.

*As you embark upon the journey that is The Template
it will be very helpful to have a sense of the connection
between the circuitry, the endocrine system and the DNA.
The DNA is the manifest blueprint from which we as Humans
and all other forms of life are constructed.
It is no secret that over 98% of our genetic material
is non-functioning. It has become a known fact that out
of the 3,000 billion base pair chemicals that make up
this code, only 60 million are active.*

***The Template codes are an intelligent patterning of information
that acts as an alchemical catalyst to activate dormant potential.***

*Contemporary physicists have discovered that this dormant genetic
material is not 'junk' DNA, as put forward by orthodox science,
but is in fact a living data storage system, a library of Human
potential which, when unlocked and resurrected, will put an end
to suffering, disease, conflict and death itself – rendering
the Human a fully realized, conscious entity able to access
any time or energy level in the universe.*

*Transcendence/ascension must and will include the reversal
of this genetic mutation/modification to resurrect the complete
Human code. This code is present in its fullness within
the Soul Covenant, embedded in the Human matrix,
and lying dormant in the disconnected DNA filaments.*

*It is the reconnection of bio-circuitry that will deliver
the life-force energy that will ultimately resurrect these codes.*

Bio-circuitry and Resurrection

*At this time, the Human unit of circuitry is not capable
of sustaining its molecular structure in a state
of super-consciousness or enlightenment, as many of its major
circuits are disconnected, resulting in an insufficient supply
of electromagnetic input. It is this subtle energy supply
that animates the Human being on every level.*

**The energetic nature of consciousness that fosters all life
is integrated by the Human heart/ body/mind via the bio-circuitry.
The circuitry is the delivery system that integrates
this Source Intelligence, translating this energetic
electromagnetic life-force into the bio-informational matrix
that is the vibratory infrastructure of the Human hologram.**

*The circuitry, however, does not begin and end around the Human
energy field. Each circuit is in fact spherical and intersects
with another spherical field of conscious energy, which, in turn,
interacts with another, as part of an electromagnetic intelligence
system that encompasses all - from the subatomic
to the multi-universal, the wheels within wheels.*

*Each sphere of consciousness is a holonomic fractal
of Source Intelligence. The Source is everywhere.
The more circuitry the Human entity is able to utilize within its
computational system, the more Source Intelligence it is able
to integrate and synthesize, and the more conscious
and enlightened that entity becomes.*

*Enlightenment is not simply a state in which the intellect
is in possession of questions and answers - it is a state of being
in which the full spectrum of Source Consciousness is integrated,
synthesized and crystallized into the incarnate body presence,
understood in the mind, felt in the heart
and made tangible in the body.*

*Transcendence/ascension is resurrecting the dormant components
within the Human hologram, to be embraced back into the
governing mechanism of the universal holography.*

The Endocrine System

*As the energetic nature of consciousness begins its journey through
the circuitry, it triggers bio-informational signals that stimulate the
endocrine system to function according to the degree of 'intelligence'
being integrated. The degree of dataflow is reliant upon the number
of circuits connected in order to deliver this intelligence code
and the endocrine system's ability to decipher and utilize its signals.
This is a vital symbiotic relationship, as the endocrine system
is a stepping-stone between Source Intelligence and the Human
ability to translate that data into life experience
and to know itself as eternal.
The endocrine system is the sacred interface between
the life directive transmitted from Source and the Human
manifestation of that directive on all levels.*

*As the circuitry delivers this electromagnetic consciousness,
the chakra centers act as transducers of the energy, stepping it
down into absorbable data for the entire body system to utilize,
emotionally, physically and mentally.*

*The relationship between the circuitry, the endocrine glands,
the chakras, the DNA and the point of soul evolution
is an impeccably interactive and co-creative one, organically
regulated by each individual's capacity for change.*

*Light
is the radiant
Emissary of the
Benevolence
of Creation*

Light and the Pineal

*Understanding the role and function of the pineal will greatly clarify
the connection between circuitry, the endocrine system
and the resurrection of the original Human design
prior to genetic modification.
It is this gland that is responsible for the absorption,
translation and distribution of light as information.*

*Due to the modification of the DNA and the disconnection of circuitry,
this magical gland is in atrophy as it has been separated
from its life-force energy supply.*

Light is the radiant Emissary of the Benevolence of Creation.

*Constructed of retinic cells, as are the eyes, the pineal encases
a series of lenses that mirror and translate light into data
for the body's bio-informational system to utilize. The more
electromagnetic life-force the body system is integrating
(through the reconnection of circuitry), the more the endocrine system
receives in order to rejuvenate, and the more light can be translated
and utilized. This form of 'light in translation' is distributed through
the central nervous system and into the DNA. At this time the atrophy
of the pineal renders it capable of translating only a limited spectrum
of light, a spectrum that ensures the survival and procreation
of the Human race but little more. As the pineal is rejuvenated via
the reconnection of circuitry and the acceleration of electromagnetic
input, it absorbs and translates further spectrums of light.*

*As this light reaches the DNA as Source Intelligence, it creates
a cellular resonance with the light-encoded disconnected genetic
material. This expanded spectrum of light holds the immortal code
of the universal matrix for which there is a dormant
counter-resonant code present within the disconnected
genetic material that lies within every cell.*

*The reconnection of circuitry is fundamental
to the transmutation of the life/death/rebirth cycle.*

*The present mortal life span of Humanity is a resonant response
to bio-informational signals that initiate the decline of vital energies
through aging into physical death. The signals can be traced
to the ratio of chemicals in the brain/blood. These chemicals
are manufactured by the endocrine system. The endocrine system
functions according to the life-force being supplied by the **circuitry**.*

*Due to the disconnection of circuitry the endocrine system
is in atrophy and is producing a hormonal composition
that is in resonance with the present fear-based,
dualistic perception of reality - and physical death.*

*As circuitry is reconnected, the endocrine system is reunited
with its vital energy supply and each organ is rejuvenated
to its original life-enforcing function. It then begins to create
an altered body chemistry that transmits the bio-informational signals
resonant with the immortal paradigm - hormonal elixirs of eternal life.*

*The new paradigm will be birthed into time and space through
the **embodiment** of the creation frequency as we reconnect
electromagnetically to the **Source** through
the reconnection of circuitry.*

Frequency, Resonance and the Morphogenetic Field

When you reconnect a circuit, you return the energetic nature of consciousness to the arena presided over by that circuit. This energetic intelligence is electromagnetic and it is this electromagnetism that substantiates the wave patterns of frequency. The frequency is the shape of the wave. It is these frequency wavelengths that dictate the dimensional paradigms of existence.

Everything is frequency... frequency is consciousness emanating from Source. The primal pathways utilized by frequency to express the intelligence of Source Consciousness are geometric. (The geometric nature of consciousness is explored in 'The Sacred Geometry of The Template').

*As you reconnect circuitry, you accelerate the frequency input of Source Intelligence into the incarnate body presence, recalibrating your vibrational resonance with the resonance of creation (see 'Circuitry, DNA and The Endocrine System'). You vibrate at a higher frequency, a frequency that integrates new spectrums of Source Intelligence, a benevolent vibration - **love**.*

Just as the pure Human instinct is to reach out and bond through love, the primal drive of frequency is to search for a like frequency with which to resonate. As these resonant frequency waveforms embrace and share information they form a grid of unified frequency, a web of consciousness. It is the weave of these tapestries of resonance that dictates the fabric of realities.

Circuitry and the Unified Resonant Field

*As individuals, initiates will immediately experience
a degree of transformation, physically, emotionally and mentally
as a result of the reconnection of circuitry. When a circuit is tested
through kinesiology or muscle testing, the renewed strength that is
experienced in the test-point is an indication on the physical level
of the change that has taken place on all levels. How and when
this change manifests in the individual is a question of their
ability to embrace it. Everything about that individual
is taken into consideration - their present emotional state,
their astrology and life circumstances.*

*Collectively the growth in the numbers of connected units
of circuitry triggers the transformational acceleration
of the individual as the collective consciousness is shared
through resonant frequency.*

*As initiates reconnect circuitry, altering their frequency
through acceleration of electromagnetic life-force into their
'bio-computer', their altered vibrational transmission reaches out
for a like frequency with which to resonate. In this way
the family of initiates support each other through vibration.
Acceleration through association occurs as initiates gather together
in conscious groupings and their vibrational support magnifies
and multiplies through resonance.*

*As the number of initiates grows, so too does the unified
resonant field of shared frequency, of shared holistic consciousness.
As a number of reconnected units of circuitry reach critical mass,
their unified resonant field finds a new stability:
a new morphogenetic field.*

**The morphogenetic field is the bio-spheric containment
of the resonant field of shared consciousness.**

*This resonant field of shared consciousness is co-dependent
and interactive with the Human behavioral reference points
that reside within the archetypal arena. The archetypal arena
is nourished and defined by the quality of consciousness
derived from Source Intelligence.*

*As initiates integrate an acceleration of consciousness through
the reconnection of circuitry, archetypal reference points
within the psyche are nourished and redefined in resonance
with the Benevolence of Creation that is the Source Intelligence.*

*This archetypal redefinition of Source is a frequency.
When this frequency is shared by a critical mass of units of circuitry,
it will create a substantiation of transcendental consciousness
that will stabilize the new morphogenetic field... a new bio-spheric
field of Source Intelligence ... a new consciousness grid.*

*The morphogenetic field is intrinsic to the evolution of Human
consciousness on a global scale. It is an interactive fractal
within the hyper-hologram of manifest creation, drawing into its
holonomic mechanism the many intricate systems that together
weave the implicate order of our existence - our endocrine systems,
chakra systems, neuro-biology, even our Souls' Covenant.
Our every thought affects this field of consciousness.*

*As you reconnect more and more circuits you will begin
to resurrect an innate comprehension of the holonomic
system that ties your consciousness into this field
of consciousness...into the Sun, the stars,
and the center of the galaxy.*

*The journey
of liberation begins
with needlessness
as a state of total
sentient sovereignty
is realized*

Vegetarianism

The journey of liberation begins with needlessness as a state of total sentient sovereignty is realized.

As we begin to reconnect circuitry and resurrect the original Human blueprint, we integrate and synthesize a natural resonance with the Benevolent Source of Creation. As this resonance gradually and harmoniously infiltrates every level of consciousness we will begin to redefine the way in which we sustain ourselves. Physically, we will no longer be able to sustain our molecular structure by the taking of life in any form as the Human matrix is altered through heightened awareness of its interconnectedness with all creation. Energy will then be directly assimilated through Sacred Breath as we internally manufacture, in the alchemical laboratory of the Human temple, elixirs of eternal life. This will not happen through intellectual direction alone but through the harmonious unfolding of organic alignments radiating out from our inner core. With more and more reconnected circuitry we will integrate more and more of the Source Consciousness that supports our desire to become harmless and needless.

"Whosoever eats of the flesh of slain beasts, eats of the body of death."
The Essene Gospel of Peace

The planetary frequency is becoming more and more dense as we move closer to the pinnacle of the precession of the equinoxes. Simultaneously the periphery of a new reality, a new model of existence, a new paradigm, is forming the counter-balance for this acceleration of the shadow. Many of us are living in both worlds.

This transitional phase is a great and testing challenge. To stabilize this new paradigm when all around, the prevailing frequencies of fear oppose you, is exhausting. The physical body has to deal with many new chemicals and a barrage of fear-inducing global insanities that are disturbing our hormonal balance. Negative manipulation of consciousness through media is accelerating daily. Food has lost the integrity of its infrastructure as it becomes undermined by the use of chemicals inescapable in the air and water, and hugely by genetically modified seed banks.

There is less and less resonance with the food supply as not only is it becoming less digestible, but our resonance with a greater spectrum of light is lessening our resonance with the archaic process of gross consumption...the buying, cooking, eating, eliminating process. Our conscious evolution is preparing us on deep levels to embrace a direct assimilation of pure energy.

Consuming flesh substantiates the death resonance defiling the sacred enclosure of the body-temple.

Even those who have for many years abstained from the consumption of flesh are mistaking their feelings of exhaustion and desire for nourishment as a lack of flesh protein. Many are grounding themselves into a reality that is stabilized by fear, by eating fear. As death approaches, the animal chosen for slaughter moves quickly into 'fight or flight' mode, releasing massive amounts of adrenaline into its muscular structure in order to stimulate the strength and speed it will need to escape its killer. When this toxic substance is ingested it stimulates the reptilian brain to trigger exaggerated aggression responses. Adrenal toxicity accelerates the degeneration of the physical body.

When ingesting slain flesh you are, without doubt, involved in, and responsible for, not only the death of the animal but also its suffering. The inescapable, inherent sense of guilt triggers deep denial and the subjugation of compassion that dulls the senses, creating paranoid self-revulsion neurosis, substantiating the hopelessness of your own separation from the continuum. There is little point in cleansing your chakras with crystals and clearing your spaces with incense when you continue to defile your body-temple with slain flesh.

This is not a moral issue - it is one of balance. No amount of positive thinking or 'blessings' can correct the imbalance. You cannot expect to fully enjoy and receive that which you take... life. A friend argued this point with me one day. "In this world" he said, "in order for something to live, something must die". This of course is one of the balance mechanisms that maintain duality. The choice is yours... do you wish to remain within this realm of conflict and suffering...in which reality do you want to ground your resonance?

*A vegetarian/vegan diet is the first step in transcending the gross
tendencies that govern our dualistic existence. Ideally it is preferable
to make this decision from your own inner realizations and the voice
of compassion in your heart rather than from guilt or shame.
However, if you cannot hear that voice,
become a vegetarian and you will.*

*The reconnection of circuitry will assist this move
away from one of Humanity's darkest and deepest addictions
by reconnecting the energy supply to the endocrine system
and redefining the way in which we sustain life, not through
an adopted discipline, but from the harmonious unfoldment
of organic alignments radiating from our core...from the heart.*

*Ultimately we shall be sustained by light and love when we can fully
resonate with the complete mandala of the immortal paradigm
gifted to us by the Benevolent Source of Creation.
Until then it is vital to begin to make the changes within
our lives that are within our reach.*

The Sun
is the mediator
of Prime Intelligence
between ourselves
and Galactic
Consciousness

Immortality

Eternal life is not desired, nor is death feared... within the immortal paradigm these issues simply do not exist.

It is the subject of immortality that confounds many of those who come to The Template workshops, for the death program is deep and all pervading. However, physical immortality is not so new and outrageous a concept as you might think.

Taoists have long believed that physical immortality can be attained through continuous physical rejuvenation. The Taoist system sees this rejuvenation occurring through the activation of the life-giving properties of hormones through sexual stimulation. Various factions of Tibetan Buddhism teach Anapanasati, *the practice of 'mindful breathing' that can lead to liberation from disease and death. Both these concepts - continual rejuvenation and mindful breathing - are components within The Template system of transcendence of the mortal paradigm.*

In The Template system, it is the reconnection of circuitry that instigates the resurrection of the entire endocrine system, the pranic mechanism and the Soul Covenant, activating and integrating the dormant genetic material that ultimately leads to physical immortality. It is not that The Template model is an immortalist movement, focusing on that outcome as its prime objective; it is the resurrection of the original Human blueprint and the realignment of the incarnate body presence with the natural dataflow of the life-directive that emanates from the omnipotent Heart of Creation.

The natural order of this life continuum is endless and eternal, without beginning or end. The physical deterioration that leads to the death of the manifest expression of life that is the body is the result of an unnatural deficit of life-force that has occurred as a result of our disconnection from that continuum.

Physical immortality is not a miraculous state of being -
it is the natural embodiment of the Benevolence of Creation,
a reunification with our quintessential identity that is defined
by our connection to Source. It is important and immensely
empowering to begin to see immortality as your natural state
that is simply lying dormant and awaiting the various decisions
you will make to awaken your immortal self.

In Taoist belief, the kidney system, in particular the supradrenal
glands or adrenal cortex are cited as the regulators of the sexual
potency that leads to the physical rejuvenation required for
immortality. In The Template, the circuitry reconnected in all
the Ceremonies leads to the rejuvenation of not only these glands
but the entire endocrine system. It is imperative for integrated
and sustainable rejuvenation that the organs are not considered
in isolation but as a whole system. To treat an isolated organ
and focus on that inevitably leads to imbalance.

Circuitry draws the heart/mind/body system into the nurture
of the holonomic life-giving mechanism
that begins in the Benevolent Heart of Creation.

The endocrine system must be kept in the loop of continual
rejuvenation regardless of sexual activity or intellectual discipline.
With layer upon layer of the life-sustaining energy system reinstated
through reconnection of circuitry, the primal infrastructure
of the core Human blueprint is stabilized allowing the rejuvenating
force of rising kundalini to be integrated and synthesized
by the heart/body/mind system.

Sexuality is realized as the most sacred divine function
of the original Human, not only as a source of pleasure
and rejuvenation but as the realization of the God/Goddess potency
that defines us as universal progenitors of life.
Sexual activity then occurs not with an end in mind but,
as the result of a natural divine passion originating
from a core desire to celebrate and share love.

The Quantum Leap

The Immortal Template exists within the Soul Covenant embedded in the Human matrix.

Immortality. We are not speaking here of the lengthening of the life span. Such concepts become moot, dissolving into inconsequentiality against the the magnificence of a fully resurrected original Human. If Humanity understood the fine membrane that exists between themselves and death, the word itself would not evoke such dread and fear! This dread looms behind each thought, dwells within each breath, the day that comes to separate every mother and child, every lover from the last kiss.
We are not speaking here of the laboratory temples in which man defeats death with intelligence to preserve the flesh that bit longer. We are talking of transcending the morphogenetic limitation that defines the parameters of the mortal paradigm - Human/planetary transcendence.

Transcendence of the mortal paradigm requires critical mass.

In order to achieve and stabilize this quantum leap into the immortal paradigm, a planetary resonant field of a stable frequency is required, a frequency that is created and stabilized by a numerical mass of resurrected units of bio-circuitry translating and transmitting the full spectrum of the creative directive emanating from Source, providing new archetypal reference points in the collective neural membrane that is the morphogenetic field, breaking the spell of the mortal trance and reconnecting the planetary bio-sphere to the immortal continuum.

It is difficult, if not impossible, for individuals to sustain an immortally relevant degree of mutation within their genetic codes, their DNA, without the reinforcement of a sympathetic morphogenetic field. Otherwise they would find themselves in a different dimension, for we have a 'symbiotic covenant' embedded in the Human matrix that defines us as functioning fractals of the universal holography.

*The sentient body of this planet Earth has, embedded in every leaf
and blade of grass, a holonomic covenant that is co-creative
and interactive with this Human Soul Covenant. Whatever conscious
evolvement takes place within the alchemical crucible of the Human
unit of circuitry is out-pictured in the eco-cosmic environment.
Transcendence will not take place on a space ship, but within the
materialized co-ordinates that are the space/time ship... Earth.
In order to realize this Human/planetary transcendence
there must be critical mass.*

The Sun and Immortality

*Mortality is not only substantiated by the obvious - our lack
of genetic material and the psychosocial, chemical, religious
and electromagnetic manipulation of our consciousness - but also
by our deficient morphic resonance with the solar system
and by our inability to translate light.*

*At this time, planet Earth is trapped in a frequency band of extreme
oscillation of magnetic influence that is disturbing the natural solar
equilibrium, the subconscious matrix of archetypal reference and our
ability to embrace the full spectrum of the Source Intelligence
transmitted by the Sun.*

*The Sun represents to our psyche the most comprehensive monadic
configuration that triggers the geometric Soul Covenant and imbues
our physical matrix with the immortal frequency.
This lack of solar resonance is being stabilized by a foreign body
within our solar system. This synthetic influence is triggering
a chemical imbalance in the Human brain, creating a narcotic dream
state in which we are experiencing continual disempowerment
as we play out our fear, shame and guilt scenarios.*

*This is an important and vital aspect of the arrested conscious
development of the Human race and its addiction to conflict,
and will be investigated in the second Template workbook.
The 5th Ceremony (The Temple of Time Ceremony) reconnects
the circuits of time/space co-ordinates that will assist
in the reinstatement of our resonance with the entire solar system,
as we become the map and the calendar.*

*Due to the mutant space/time continuum of the present frequency
zone, Humanity is tied into a cycle of degeneration with the passing
of each year as the Earth circles the Sun. The Sun, the giver of life,
instead counts off these increments of 'time' that define
our journey towards the grave. In this way the Sun
has become the hourglass of death.*

*In the Ceremonies of Activation and Integration the Soul Covenant
embedded in the Human matrix is activated and integrated.
A component within the alchemical code that triggers this
is the presence and use of the geometric 'solar-spheric fractals'
of the 3rd dimensional hologram. Our ability to comprehend,
within our psyches, the primary seed of creation, the Monad,
represented in Earth's solar system as the Sun, is redefined.*

*The Sun is reinstated as the mediator of Prime Intelligence
between ourselves and Galactic Consciousness.*

*The Sun no longer holds us to ransom... no longer does each sunrise
and sunset provide the demarcation of a passively accepted span
of consciousness creating a strictly defined parameter in which
we must organize our short existence.*

*Now, with the activation and integration of our solar-spheric
resonance, a labyrinth of cosmic comprehension is opening to us,
within us. Every ray of light becomes the definition of endlessness...
sealing, within the Human matrix, life eternal.*

**As this light, newly understood, synthesizes within the body
crucible, our physical matrix is imbued with the Tantric Amrita
of spirit and matter - the birth of immortality.**

*Ceremony
is the mechanism
through which
what you know
becomes
who you are*

Ceremony

The mechanism through which what you know becomes who you are.

In this age of mass communication, our deepest fears are mirrored and continually projected into our daily lives by extensive media feedback, fed through the Human psyche via literature, films and round-the-clock news, infiltrating our dream states and reinforcing demonic archetypal reference points within the morphogenetic field. Thus the consensus fabric of fear-based reality is woven by our very thought processes. Our pathological compliance within this reality can be tracked back to the modification of our genetic coding, the disturbance of our morphic resonance with the solar system and our resultant inability to translate the full spectrum of light.

The rectification of this Human/global predicament cannot be achieved by direct action. You cannot affect the fountain of life by disturbing its waters; you must adjust the fountainhead from which this life springs. To fight for freedom is to embody the struggle.

"The problems we have cannot be solved at the same level of thinking with which we created them."
Albert Einstein

To psychoanalyze our problems is to utilize a solution that exists at the level of the problem, for our analytical skills evolve from a brain 4/5 of which is inactive. Nothing less than the resurrection of the original Human genetic code will break the consensus spell of our dualistic perception.

Ceremony is the solution that exists outside of the problem.

Ceremonies are codes. They are an alchemical patterning of holistic intelligence that invoke, through resonance, new patterns of response within the cerebral cortex, creating powerful brain chemistry that unfetters the intellect from its dogmatic space-time parameters, opening a gateway into a limitless continuum.

The Cerebral Cortex - the Temple of Remembrance

The shift of focus to the cerebral cortex denies the reptilian brain monopoly over conscious perception. The over-stimulation of the reptilian brain is a condition that is being stimulated and stabilized by the worldwide fear-based socio-political, self-perpetuated 'terrorist' concerns that dominate the communication media, by the erroneous archetypal definition of Source/God through religion, the consuming of slain flesh and the retardation of the Human ability to translate light... to name but a few. This manipulation of frequency is galvanizing within the collective psyche a desperate sense of shame and guilt, emotions that calibrate at the same frequency as death. The reptilian brain dominance is triggering adrenal toxicity, a powerful hormonal imbalance that is causing a myriad of physical, mental and emotional diseases.

As you will discover in the Actualization phase of The Template, the cerebral cortex is the Temple of Remembrance that holds the innocence of the original Human blueprint prior to genetic modification. This blueprint defines the Human entity as an 'Emissary of Source': the God/Goddess potency. As the arena of reference for this identity, the cerebral cortex, is stimulated through Ceremony (and through the reconnection of The Temple of Remembrance Circuit), the quintessential Human definition is reaffirmed, not only intellectually but physically, emotionally and hormonally, through the influx of the electromagnetic life-force system that carries the immortal harmonic, in resonance with the original Human blueprint.

The alchemical combination inherent within a coded Ceremony reaches deeper than psychoanalysis and galvanizes a new behavioral concordance within the archetypal arena of the psyche. Rather than trying to adopt a new behavioral 'sanity' through an intellectual idea of it, the Ceremonies are alchemical affirmations that celebrate the inherent perfection that resides in the innocent heart of each Human, raising the desired model of Human behavior out of the intellectual arena and into the field of experience.

Resurrection Through Sound

*The modification of our DNA was not perpetrated via the use
of laboratory technology alone, but also through sound. It is sound
that will return to us the magnificence of our original design.
Looking into the 98% of disconnected material within the DNA,
Russian scientists have begun to understand that this is not "junk"
DNA as orthodox science would have us believe. It holds the same
properties and abilities as the percentage of DNA that is now being
used. They have discovered that this dormant material is a language
that will respond to a 'resonant language'. They stress, however,
that this language must hold the 'correct frequency'. In The Template
Ceremonies, the linguistic code is patterned in such a way as to create
this required resonant frequency. The content, structure and cadence
of the sonic linguistic code accessed in the Ceremonies hold a fractal
harmonic of the creation code present within the Soul Covenant.*

*Although DNA modification has altered the helix and endocrine
function, the light-code of the full Human magnificence is out of the
reach of manipulation and exists in its entirety, holographically, in our
every cell. To resurrect this original blueprint that is the light body,
we create a mirror waveform of its intelligence, to entice it back
into this frequency zone through resonance... through Ceremony.*

*We have discovered, through collaboration with the Consciousness
that represents The Template Ceremonies, that it is not only the
resonance of sound that is necessary to resurrect the dormant DNA;
the divine sense of sight* and the visual embrace of the elemental
components of the creation matrix are also required within
the alchemy to catalyze the sonic code and stabilize transformation.
Thus the manifest presence of the geometric elemental components
of creation; Water, Air, Earth, Fire, Ether and Stellar Radiance
are an alchemical presence at the Ceremonies, not merely upon paper
or on a computer screen but objectified in real space-time.*

*The Template Ceremonies are an animated, alchemical mandala
that create the mirror waveform of the creation frequency.
The interference pattern between the original Human blueprint
and the Ceremony code conceives a Vesica Piscis through
which the original Human hologram is resurrected.*

---

* *Those who suffer from any form of sense deficiency such as blindness are afforded
a special dispensation.*

Phase I

Foundation

*The Reconnection
of the 12 Basal Circuits*

**The Ceremony
of Original Innocence**

Original Innocence
The Child

*The first Ceremony reconnects the 12 basal circuits, taking
you back to the first choice, prior to your first breath, propelling
you into a sense of yourself as creator rather than victim.
Life is not happening to you but because of you - you stand
in the center: generating, orchestrating and
choreographing every movement.
The key to this shift in perception is forgiveness. To embrace
forgiveness is to embody the living mandala of love upon which
is based the fundamental Human ethic. As you forgive,
you shed the first layer of mortality.
You have reached the very depth of your ability to forgive
when you realize that there is nothing to forgive.*

*For many, the need to forgive begins in the womb and during birth,
but mostly in the first five years of childhood. There are no more
powerful words than 'Mother' and 'Father'.*

*While living in Hawaii, I took my two-year old son to the top of
a mountain to watch the Sun setting into the ocean. He sat in perfect
silent stillness until the great golden orb disappeared completely.
Turning to me with wonder in his eyes, he said, "Do that again
Mum." In that moment I saw the magnitude of the trust and faith
he had in me, and the deep iconic position that every parent holds
within the psyche of their children, and the power of that position.
As universal progenitors of life we, as men and women,
as mothers and fathers, are the incarnate emissaries
of the Benevolence of Creation - Gods and Goddesses.
The impact we have on our children is incalculable.
Within The Template system of transcendence the
healing of this relationship is paramount and is the first
step taken within the journey of resurrection.*

*This healing is not only emotional - it begins at the fulcrum point
within the archetypal arena of the psyche, ultimately affecting
the DNA. Through the alchemical catalyst of Ceremony, a new point
of compassionate reference is created in which initiates embrace
a level of forgiveness that transcends blame, guilt and shame as they
take full responsibility for their decision to enter conceptual existence
and, by so doing, understand that all behavior makes perfect sense,
and that all experience simply adds to the perfection of who they are.
This is done trans-personally within the context
of Sacred Ceremony: personal details are not entered into.*

*Suddenly, suffering is seen as that which
"shatters the shell around your understanding". **

*That which once seemed like a destructive trauma
becomes the gift.*

* *From "The Prophet" by Kalil Gibrahn*

To embrace forgiveness
is to embody
the living mandala
of love
upon which is based
the fundamental
Human ethic

Forgiveness

*Forgiveness is the most fundamental forward movement
towards the integration of light and shadow within.
Without it we run aground in the stagnant waters
of judgment and denial. Forgiveness is you co-operating
with the impeccability of creation, accelerating
your conscious evolution.*

*To forgive is to marry agony and ecstasy and to glimpse
the divine plot in all its glorious perfection.*

Forgiveness is knowing there is nothing to forgive.

*It is forgiveness that reconnects the Water and Air circuits.
Its alchemical function in the Ceremony instigates a dynamic
that employs not only emotional and intellectual reasoning
but reaches the fountainhead of behavior, the DNA, setting up new
neural pathways. Forgiveness changes the chemical balance
within the Human brain. In this way the electromagnetic field
then holds a resonant support system for forgiveness,
creating an inner dialogue of compassion.*

*When you forgive, you embrace absolutely your 'response–ability'
in the interconnectedness of all creation. Synchronicity reveals
more of itself. This life is not happening to you but because of you.
You stand in the center, generating, orchestrating
and choreographing every movement.*

*Forgiveness is an emotional, intellectual and biological signal sent
to yourself, that you understand that all behavior makes perfect sense.
Every interaction becomes a mirror reality, for it is the mirror,
the watery element of reflection that breaks the spell of blame.*

*In using a mirror in the Ceremony, a conduit of consciousness
is established through the eye and its infinite ability
to reflect back and forth, like placing mirror to mirror.*

(Partners can use each other's eyes instead of the mirror).

*This infinite reflection reaches through the windows of the soul,
beyond the space-time continuum, into the past and the future.
A chemical pattern of deep receptivity is arranged in the brain
and an overriding decision is inserted. A resonant pattern
of response that resides in the original Human design
greets, enforces and establishes it.*

*Forgiveness is not a selective choice but a way of being.
Can you say I shall forgive this but that is unforgivable?
To deem anyone unforgivable is to stand in opposition to the
Omnipotent Heart of Creation, from which springs forth ALL.*

From Victim to Creator

*The gateway to the path that leads to the transmutation of the
life/death/rebirth cycle is opened through a deep understanding
of forgiveness and is the shedding of the first layer of mortality,
initiating the journey from victimhood to creatorship.*

*It is the transitional phases of the birth and culmination
of any cycle that hold the points of power which create the space
for transformation. If this moment is grasped in full consciousness,
nothing is ever seen the same again. The heart soars as the soul
experiences that first taste of liberation. The deterioration at the end
of a cycle is as important as its conception. The notion of rebelling
against the degenerative phase is preposterous. What is called
for is an understanding of this movement within the dance and an
honoring of the divine plan that moves the age onwards to its demise
as it has thousands of times before and will again and again.
It is not for us to fight its ending, but to see ourselves within its flow,
to come to know our own individual cycles, to feel the tongue-and-
groove of our genetic codes and to know how they fit effortlessly
into the wheel of eternal existence, bringing us into line with our
reason for being here, now - coming into and taking part
in the orgasmic nature of the cosmos.*

*We are not here to repair the degenerative phase of this age,
but to harness the powerful energies of culmination to create a pure
burst of conception. The ultimate 'conspiracy' behind this phase
of our world age is one of love in perfect balance with wisdom ...
a love that allows for experience and free will.*

58

*As you continue to resist that which you perceive as injustice,
that injustice will continue to persist as part of your perception.
It may be time to scrutinize the deceptions being perpetrated upon
this planet but it is never time to hold on to fear, anger or grief,
for these emotions will tarnish your intentions and defile your
inspiration. Allow yourself to see perfection even where you have
been convinced it does not exist and you will begin to integrate
and synthesize within yourself the light and the shadow,
moving more easily beyond the addictive illusions of duality.*

*Welcome the signs of decay as the milestones of Humanity's
deliverance into another realm of existence free of duality.
Cultivate in your heart acceptance, gratitude and appreciation
and they will bring you the bliss of peace - filling your Human
embodiment with the grace and refinement that is the
birthright and inheritance of your race as it operates
within its original state of grace... innocence.*

*The overview of the present day predicament of Humanity is of a new
seed race rising out of the rotting fruit of its past history. A steel blade
emerges strengthened from the countless beatings of the blacksmith's
hammer in the heat of the forging fire. We have come here, through
our own transformational energy, to gestate and give birth to a new
planet... together. However, this new planet reclines gloriously in the
future, dressed not in the tattered hand-me-downs of a patched-up
world age, but in a gown spun with gossamer threads of a new vision,
springing from the heart of Humanity, from the great loom of a new
frequency grid-work – an altogether separate reality.*

*Is it not true that as the desecration and destruction of this world age
march on with ever more fervor, we are more willing to surrender
to the loss of it? More willing to wake up and dream it anew,
to engage the radical mutation within our Human bio-circuitry
that will accommodate, anchor and transmit the higher frequencies
needed to create the springboard for the quantum leap.
It is no use to take up arms against the sea of madness, for the insane
perpetrators of the impending holocaust are caught up in a cycle
that is alive and must die a natural death. You have not come
here to experience this holocaust but to ingest, integrate
and transmute the apparent poisons of this world age.*

*Seeing all things as equal is the transforming element within the brew
to be used by you, the alchemists of the coming age of balance.
For without that understanding, judgment knocks you
out of the realm of cosmic consciousness. It is all a mirror for you
to look into, to see and feel what disempowerment and control can
look and feel like. It is there to inspire you with great passion to
become the embodiment of freedom. As you forgive and understand
those who have separated you from that freedom, simultaneously
realizing your connectedness to all creation, you forgive yourself;
empowering your thoughts with the knowledge that
you are the source generating all experiences that you have,
stepping out of the victimhood that has led to the co-operation
of our race in its own destruction, and stepping into creatorship.
Become the silent witness not only of your personal dramas
allowing you to "shuffle off this mortal coil" but also to the shamanic
death of a culture that is fast reaching the nadir of its rotting history.*

*Align yourself with the new seed!
It is time to wake up and start dreaming a new dream.
Impregnate it with your original innocence.*

*Only the one who looks down and sees that it is truly her hands
gripping the helm can navigate her way through the stormy
pirate-infested waters of free will and choice.*

*The chapter "Forgiveness" is from
"Original Innocence - The Reconnection of Human Bio-Circuitry
Through Coded Ceremony" by Juliet Carter*

*Circuitry
is the delivery system that
integrates Source Intelligence
translating this energetic
electromagnetic life-force
into the bio-informational matrix
that is the vibratory infrastructure
of the Human hologram*

Foundation

*Spirit draws near the Earth and enters matter through the stargate
created by the union between the male and female potencies.
The geometric Soul Covenant written in the language of light
appears on the etheric to hold the blueprint of another being
entering the conceptual world of Earth.*

*In the womb of Woman life begins. In the rich, red, warm darkness
is felt the first element ... **Water**.*

*Through the initiation of birth comes the second element of **Air**
as the first breath, the bridge to consciousness,
is given and taken.*

*The first breath activates the independent electromagnetic field
of circuitry, instantaneously coded by the geomagnetic field
of the Earth and the Galaxy. This astrologically imprints the Human
co-ordinates within time and space. Through this resonance
the third element of **Earth** imprints the senses.*

*The Earth circles the Sun and as the years pass, a growing
passion builds as the fourth element of **Fire** is fanned by desire.*

*When that fire is tamed by an open heart and a conscious
knowledge of Source there is a return to spirit and the
fifth element of **Ether** makes light of the world.*

*The total Solar Eclipse of August 11th 1999 further seduced
the periphery of the Aquarian Age to weave its promise
of uncompromised integrity into our present reality, bringing with it
the spectrum of indigo and reactivating our inherent trust
in Ceremony, paving the way for Humanity's ability to respond
to the cosmic codes endlessly transmitted by the Galactic Core;
codes to undo the spell of history and sow the seeds
of the Galactic Human as we return to the embrace of cosmic identity.*

*The workings of The Ceremony of Original Innocence are built upon
the laws of resonant harmonics. The Ceremony, by its design
and progression, is a combination code comprised of fundamental
Galactic Human ethics that build synergy with the vibratory
infrastructure of the DNA. This creates a conduit of coherent
conscious communion through which we can, with the full
measure of our wills, affect the blueprint of who we are.
Such is the level of our present evolvement.*

*It is at this fulcrum moment in Earth's history, poised as we are
on the razor's edge between success and failure, between light
and shadow, between intellectual analysis and ancient indigenous
knowledge, that we are able to make fulcrum decisions creating
full spectrum impact upon every level of our being, making conscious
the knowledge that we are the source generating all experiences
that we have, stepping out of the pathological obedience that has led
to our victimhood, and into the light world of creatorship.*

*This time of culmination, as we near the end date of our present world
history, is being orchestrated by the stars. Such is the astronomical
line-up in our solar system and our galaxy that the friction created
by the planetary dance is opening portals of power through which
we glimpse our potential. If we can approach these gateways
in states of consciousness that allow for the vulnerability necessary
to receive a new imprinting, we are awarded by the grace
of the Omnipotent Heart of Creation, boons, gifts of mercy,
that come in the form of codes - galactic coupons.*

*Our ever-evolving ability to translate and transmit a wider spectrum
of light is dissolving the heavy mantle of frequency that has obscured
the Earth's signature from the monitoring devices of Galactic Center,
the prodigal planet returns to the galactic fold. The conduit
of coherent cosmic communion is re-established and our
Ceremonies invite, through remembrance, divine intervention.*

The creation of a new paradigm will happen through our collective
individual frequencies affecting the Human global morphogenetic
field, as the Human entity mutates into a light absorbable state,
able to embody the new energies that will break the tyranny
of consensus reality. This will require the acknowledgement of our
totality. Not only are we mental, physical and emotional beings,
we are units of circuitry, electromagnetic beings.

As we delve into this aspect of our identity we discover that 98%
of Human DNA is non-functioning. Of the 3 thousand billion base
pairs, the chemicals that make up our genes, only 60 million are
active. The scientific world refers to this as "junk" DNA.
These helixes lie on one side of the border in the battle for full
consciousness. On the other side lies the electromagnetic,
psychosocial, religious and chemical manipulation of our
frequencies, all of which conspire to maintain us as
fear and guilt motivated energy sources.

Many of you may have extricated yourselves, intermittently
and to some degree, from the net cast by the world management
team: those who have constructed a reality that, minute by minute,
day by day, threatens our survival, a reality based on
and stabilized by the decisions we make from fear.
Should you drive through any city, wander through
any supermarket, and allow your computational awareness
to register and measure the consciousness being transmitted
around you, you will witness a slave race functioning
on just enough circuitry to propagate its species.

Our ability to integrate the synthesis of light and shadow
will dictate the degree to which we can enjoy without censorship
this season of Humanity, observing without judgment the sheer
brilliance of the genius that wrote the play, the divine plot
as it twists and turns through history, to take joy in the spectacle
of matter as it dances with rainbow hues through the puppets
of form to entertain you, for indeed this world of matter is a feast
and our presence here a privilege beyond words.
Each breath is a gift that allows you to stay a little longer
to observe this grand play, full of sound and fury.

***The fundamental function of The Ceremony of Original Innocence
is to reconnect 12 basal circuits of electromagnetic force
into the Human unit of circuitry.***

*The Ceremony itself is in 5 parts relating to the 5 elements:
Water, Air, Earth, Fire and Ether.*

Water

*The Ceremony begins with Water, which reconnects the Xiphoid,
Creative and Thymus circuits. Unlike the other 9 circuits
it is possible to be born with the 3 Water circuits intact, although,
much more often than not, these circuits are disturbed during
conception, gestation, birth and childhood. During conception
if the male or female taking part in the union is subjugated in any
way, one, two or all three of these circuits can be brought down.*

*During gestation the foetus is extremely sensitive to its mother's
emotional states and thought processes. The absence of the father
is also deeply registered. Should abortion be seriously considered
this being would carry a profound sense of abandonment
until the circuits interrupted during gestation are reinstated.*

*The infant at birth, as it takes its first independent breath,
is opening all of its centers as it anticipates its imminent imprinting
by the geomagnetic field of the Earth and the stars. It is thus that it
embodies the prevailing celestial influences identified as its astrology.
In this state of profound vulnerability it is not difficult to negatively
impact its emotional body. Separation from its mother,
as happens routinely in western hospitals, can disturb
all three of these circuits.*

*During the Ceremony that reconnects these Water circuits the primal
resonant connection with the mother, father, brothers and sisters
is restored not only within the arena of this incarnation but through
the ancestral soul lineage of past and future generations,
affecting the pivotal point of the now.*

*And so the return of ancestral integrity and the deep reunion between
the self and the first manifestation of the divided aspects of the
Divine Androgynous Tantric Potency, the first female and the first*

*male ambassadors of the God/Goddess, seeps into present day
relationships. This establishes a strong and stable platform on which
to begin a deep healing process, one that will unfold organically
from your inner core. One aspect of this healing is the redistribution
of power in personal relationships. If relationships have been founded
upon the subjugation of the male or female potency they will begin
to transcend this co-dependence to become co-creative.
If the framework of a relationship, once laid bare of its dysfunction,
is no longer able to provide the infrastructure needed, it may well
dissolve. One thing it will not do is house denial.*

*Forgiveness woven together with the element of Water, represented
by the reflective nature of the mirror, is the medium through which
reconnection is made between the self and the ancestral soul lineage.
Do not underestimate the power of forgiveness. Forgiveness sheds
the first layer of mortality - we cannot fly to the stars angry.
Anger seduces us into illusion and clouds our memory of truth
as it undermines our discriminatory abilities. It ties us
to the karmic wheel of birth and death.
Forgiveness liberates us from the folly of revenge.*

*The 3rd circuit in the Water Ceremony is the Thymus circuit.
The thymus is where T-cells are manufactured. T-cells are
intelligent molecules that eavesdrop on the internal language.
If at some time during gestation, birth or childhood we are exposed
to experiences that our emotional infrastructure cannot withstand,
the thymus is disconnected.
These experiences can involve varying degrees of betrayal,
abandonment or physical abuse. At birth the vulnerable
and impressionable infant immediately registers the density
of planetary vibrations, understanding through its heightened
awareness that 300,000 children a day die of malnutrition...
that child abuse exists within the reality stabilized
by a morphogenetic field of which it has just become a part.*

*These experiences can lead to life-defeating inner dialogues to which
the T-cells respond. T-cells do not make value judgments; they simply
grant the wish for life or death by manufacturing more or less
of themselves. As we know, T-cells regulate our immune systems.
Reconnecting the Thymus circuit has a phenomenal effect
on life-defeating diseases.*

Air

The disconnection of 12 major circuits of energy within the Human bio-circuitry has impeded and impacted our every natural Human function and is intrinsically connected to the manipulation of our DNA. A vital system that has been affected profoundly is the endocrine system.

The 4 circuits included in the Air Ceremony are the Third Eye, Crown, Throat and Auric circuits. The organ in the endocrine system affected by these 4 circuits is the pineal. This organ's bio-informational system is a link between the psychic body and the nervous system and is responsible for heightened states of awareness and perception.

Not only does the pineal absorb and distribute light as information via the central nervous system and into the cells, it also acts as a transducer, stepping light down into absorbable data. As we accelerate electromagnetic input to the pineal by reinstating its full circuitry, we revitalize its structure and function as a series of organic alignments unfold its true nature. It is then able to absorb the full spectrum of light pulsating from Galactic Center via the Sun. At this time there are spectrums of light geometry that are not being picked up by our pineal gland and we are missing a part of the divine plot and who we are within it. As the pineal becomes revitalized and brings in the lost spectrums of light, they will carry with them new bands of color and new octaves that will resonate with and sing a song of remembrance to the vibratory infrastructure of our dormant codes.

As this acceleration of light enters the cells, it is greeted by the patient anticipation of trillions and trillions of light-encoded filaments that make up the 98% of our disconnected genetic material.

These filaments are coded to resonate with the full spectrum of information present in light. As the pineal is rejuvenated to its full function, it will transmit to these filaments the intelligence data that will allow for the reactivation of this dormant genetic material, ultimately culminating in the cellular mutation necessary to resurrect the Transcendental Human.

Earth

The Earth circuit enters the body at the medulla oblongata and then circles around and enters 16 to 18 inches into the Earth. It is this circuit that reconnects life-force to the pituitary/hypothalamus/pineal complex. This complex is an alchemical laboratory that manufactures our neuro-chemicals and neuro-transmitters, setting the subtle ratios that determine the recipe of our hormonal elixirs and their bio-informational signals. These signals trigger resonant receptors within the Human matrix, which in turn set in motion the cogs and wheels of our deepest unconscious programs, programs that instigate and perpetuate the deterioration of the physical body. It is in this complex that we establish the neuro-chemical patterning that weaves the web of addiction.

Our lives are rooted in and overrun by addictions that infiltrate almost every impulse, thought-process and action. We cannot extricate ourselves from this predicament without a stable support system. The process of moving out of habitual response patterns and into non-dual conscious perception cannot be directed by the intellect alone. We must reconnect the circuits and create the neuro-pathways that support our move away from our addictions, stabilizing the deprogramming process.

At this time we share a morphogenetic field with those who instigate and carry out ethnic cleansing and set our watches to the same measure of time that wakes the generals from their slumber. Our seconds keep time with the marching feet of armies as 90+wars rage across the planet. Amidst all this, we can no longer chase the shallow dream of happiness, honing our abilities to maintain our ever-expanding comfort zones. We have been lulled by the hypnosis of our social and cultural conditioning to exist within lifestyles that have us flailing in a quagmire of object proliferation, weakening us into submission to addictions we are barely aware of having.

As we continue to tie our unconscious behavioral patterns into this grid we cannot redirect our instinctual impulses. To extract ourselves from our addictions we must move off this existing morphogenetic grid by beginning the process of building and stabilizing a new frequency grid-work in resonance with our original innocence.

The reconnection of the Earth circuit instigates this deprogramming/reprogramming process by establishing the beginnings of an underground grid of consciousness - a mycelium of Human awareness in the Earth and Earth awareness in the Human. As the Earth circuit is reinstated, the pituitary/hypothalamus/pineal complex is organically attuned to the crystalline core of the planet. Our pulses and impulses synchronize with our Mother and we begin to function on true free energy. This instigates a cellular renunciation of need, bringing us through organic unfoldment to our core identity and into a state of needlessness. We and the Tao become one.

When one ingests a psychedelic substance, its residue is found within the pituitary/hypothalamus/pineal complex. It is here that the ingested substance disturbs the delicate ratios that determine the balance of chemicals resonant with consensus reality. This alters the frequency waves being emitted from the brain and the visual/ audible feedback of the environment mirrors this change. We call this hallucinating. Hallucinations are not false realities, they are alternate realities tuned into as a result of a change within the chemical balance of the brain. When we revitalize the pineal/hypothalamus/pituitary complex to its original function we will be establishing a new brain chemistry, organically: a chemistry that is in resonance with the full spectrum of light. As we regain a balance within the whole unit of bio-circuitry, as a result of the reconnection of the 33 circuits through the Template Ceremonies, the revitalization of the entire endocrine system creates a new body language in resonance with the creation frequency.

As this acceleration of electromagnetic life-force pulses through the reconnected circuitry, it creates a new frequency that when vibrated by a critical mass of units of circuitry, visual/audible 'mirror feedback' will create an environment in which anything, animate or inanimate, that owes its existence to the subjugation of the male or female potencies will not be able to maintain its molecular structure.

As these changes gradually and harmoniously take place we will begin to redefine the way in which we sustain ourselves. Physically we will no longer be able to sustain our molecular structure by taking life in any form as the Human matrix is altered through heightened awareness of its inter-connectedness with all creation.

*Energy will then be directly assimilated through Sacred Breath
as we internally manufacture in the alchemical laboratory
of the body-temple, elixirs of life. This will not happen through
intellectual direction alone but through the harmonious unfolding
of organic alignments radiating from our inner core.*

*As the pituitary, hypothalamus and the pineal are resurrected
and returned to their original design we will discover our synergetic
interaction with the cosmos... understanding its influence upon us not
through historically gathered data but by direct assimilation of light.*

Fire

*The test point for the Fire circuit is situated in the perineum.
This circuit feeds the gonads, which, in tandem with the pituitary/
hypothalamus/pineal complex, manufactures the hormones that send
bio-informational signals. These in turn regulate the cyclic functions
of the reproductive system and set in motion the degenerative phase
that leads to the death of the physical body.
The present ratio of catalytic alchemical components within
this hormonal recipe gives rise to the conspiracy of mortality.
As procreation drags behind it inevitable death, love is made in fear.*

*Reconnecting the Fire circuit confronts death electromagnetically.
The knowledge that : **"never was there a time when I did not exist...
never will there come a time when I cease to be"** is no longer
only a philosophical, intellectually-adopted concept but is vibrating
its frequency at a cellular level, within the arena of the perineum.*

*Here, the acceleration of electromagnetic input is delivering the full
spectrum of the immortal harmonic, which will rejuvenate the
magical organs that define Humanity as universal progenitors of life.
When the entire endocrine system is resurrected to the fullness
of its original capabilities, it will manufacture the hormonal elixirs
that will carry to the physical matrix the full nurture
of the Benevolence of Creation... birthing physical immortality.*

*The metamorphosis from mortal to immortal will be stabilized
when our collective consciousness creates a resonant global structure
providing points of behavioral reference that allow the individual unit
of circuitry to contain and transmit the higher frequencies that will
break the tyranny of the present fear based mortal consensus.*

Ether

*Our reinstated morphic resonance with the Sun, through the reconnection of the Solar circuit, returns us to the embrace of cosmic identity. Solar Intelligence informs and vibrates the solar plexus arena, dwarfing the petty issues of our Earth dramas and the social and cultural concepts that arise from the illusions of individual supremacy. All endeavors to preserve the confines of decadent nuclear empires appear useless, empty and insane as our impulses synergize once more with the Cosmic Intelligence projected from Galactic Center and translated radiantly through our most illustrious celestial consort... the glorious **Sun**.*

It is through Humanity's reconnection to Solar and hence Galactic Intelligence that planet Earth will take Her lightfull place in the universe.

The Heart circuit is also a part of the Ether Ceremony and is situated directly above the physical heart. Its reconnection is evoked by the invitation of the purity of our souls to represent our Human expression; to embrace and empower love to take precedence over all other alliances and agendas.

The courage needed to crusade against the many apparent injustices of this world age pales against the commitment needed to face one's own shadow. The battles fought by our indigenous ancestors still rage on today but have become more sophisticated. As the spell of materialism dulls our senses, we are unable to smell the enemy as he creeps up behind us and within us. The bravest warrior with the sharpest sword is the one who can cut away all that impedes her/him from unconditional love. The battle dress of today's Servant Warrior is the seamless garb of grace and refinement that adorns the one who can integrate and synthesize the light and the shadow within.

When you have taken up enough banners and sung enough slogans and can say, "I am tired of conflict - I must leave all this sound and fury. I am ready to face the one in the mirror". It is then that the battle will truly begin... and be won.

*Removing love from the jurisdiction of attachment is the prelude
to the full acceptance that there is no separation, that all is
simultaneously one and different - to love is to be love.
Without an open heart there is nothing.*

*The Pubic circuit is the third circuit reconnected by the Ether
Ceremony and is situated at the lower tip of the pubic bone.
The dynamics that led to its disconnection are alluded to in
Genesis chapter 3 - a story more honestly told by the Sumerian texts.
The telling of the subjugation into submission of the daughters
of Eve to the appetites of an invading race of extraterrestrial beings
further outlines the genetic modification of a slave race manipulated
to perform another's bidding. We are this race. We are also
the dormant potential capable of manifesting in Human form
the full promise of our original seeding. Many different manifestations
of universal life are present upon this planet Earth.*

*Our original seeding was given by many sentient star beings
in a time of peace and was sealed by the symbol of the BIRD.
Soon we will remember, throwing off the mantle of shame
and bathing in innocence once more.*

The Elemental Components of the Ceremonial Alchemy

*The Ceremonies that together make The Template
contain within their alchemy a representation of the 5 elements:
Water, Air, Earth, Fire and Ether.*

*The 3rd and 5th Ceremonies also contain
the 6th element of Stellar Radiance.*

*Ancient traditions have acknowledged the elements as a fundamental
aspect of the healing arts, used not only in relation to the physical
body but also to maintain emotional, mental and spiritual wellbeing.
Elemental structures are now understood by modern science
to be the foundation of atomic structures.*

*In The Template Ceremonies, it is acknowledged that the Human
body-temple is constructed of this elemental intelligence.
The organizing movement of this quintessential life-giving energy
follows pathways that are geometric formulations
of the elemental frequency. The ultimate matrix that dictates the
specific geometric Human formula is the geometric Soul Covenant.
The delivery system that brings in the elemental structural
frequencies follows circuitous pathways that intersect
every level of the body system. This energy system is also known
as the meridians. The integrity of these meridians can be measured
by their strength at various points on the body surface.
As you will see from the diagrams which follow, these points
are related to the prevalent element that drives
that particular area and endocrine organ.*

*When this energy is blocked, the expression of that element and the
systems that it feeds is compromised, resulting in our being a mere
fraction of ourselves, physically, emotionally and spiritually.
When these blocks are cleared and the energy is free to flow,
a dynamic process of healing is set in motion.*

*The way in which we interface with the elements continues
to be of the utmost importance today, and is a vital aspect
of our conscious evolution.*

*Whereas various modalities, such as acupuncture, have been able
to affect these meridians to a degree and for a time, the alchemical
nature of the Ceremonies returns these energetic connections
to their natural state permanently.
The testing process of kinesiology is used before and after
Ceremonies to demonstrate the effect of reconnection of circuitry.
The Template Ceremonies give insight into the process
of our energetic connection to the manifest world
and all relationships within it.*

***The following seven pages will give you the reference points
for measuring the flow of electromagnetic energy
through the basal elemental meridians.***

The 12 Circuits

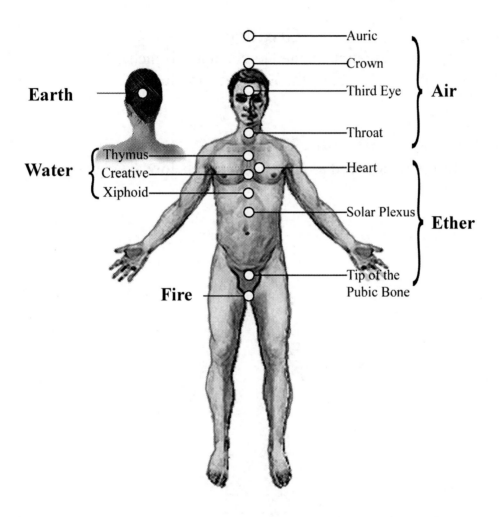

The Water Circuits

Xiphoid
Test point situated at the Xiphoid Process
(the point at which the ribs almost touch).

Creative:
Test point situated one and a half inches
above the Xiphoid Circuit.

Thymus:
Test point situated an inch and a half below the clavicle.

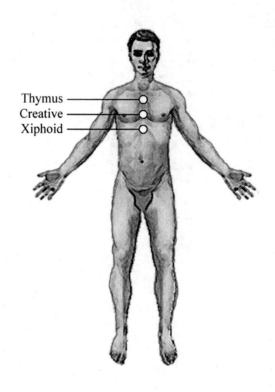

Thymus
Creative
Xiphoid

The Water Circuits

The Water circuits are disconnected during conception, gestation, birth or childhood. All the other circuits are disconnected as a result of genetic manipulation.

Xiphoid

The Xiphoid circuit is blocked by anger caused by negative interaction with a member of the same sex, most often a member of the family. This may happen as a result of physical, mental or emotional abuse. However it may also occur as a result of a lack of bonding.

Creative

The Creative circuit is blocked by guilt and regret, caused by negative interaction with a member of the opposite sex, most often a member of the family (as above).
The reconnection of this circuit has a marked effect on personal power and triggers the redistribution of power within co-dependent relationships. Relationships founded upon the subjugation of the male or female potential will either transcend or disintegrate.
As the reconnection of this circuit clears guilt there is an emancipation of creative force and an alignment with purpose.
The clearing of regret supports the release of the past and alignment with *the now*.

Thymus

The Thymus circuit is cleared spontaneously by the reconnection of the Xiphoid and Creative circuits.
The thymus gland is responsible for the production of T-cells. T-cells regulate the immune system. T-cells are intelligent molecules that eavesdrop on the internal language and grant the subconscious life or death wish. It is here that life-defeating disease begins. It is quite often the case that all three circuits are disconnected as a result of separation from the mother shortly after birth. In most hospital births, the infant is taken from the mother and placed in a fluorescent cubicle alongside other distressed infants. These first few hours of Earth experience, coming from the utterly nurturing environment of the womb, are devastating to an entirely receptive newborn.

The Air Circuits

Auric:
Situated approximately 6 inches above the head.

Crown:
Test point situated on the crown.

Third Eye:
Test point situated on the third eye.

Throat:
Test point situated at mid throat.

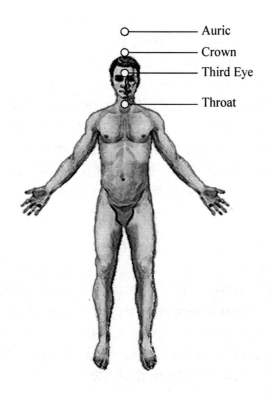

The Third Eye, Crown and Auric circuits feed the pineal gland.
The pineal gland is situated in the center of the brain and although
surrounded by grey matter is responsible for the absorption of light.
Light is distributed through the central nervous system into every cell
and all DNA. The re-introduction of electromagnetic input to the pineal
will rejuvenate this gland and thus it will absorb more light – light
to which the disconnected helixes are coded to respond.

The Earth Circuit

Earth:
Test point situated in the center of the medulla oblongata.

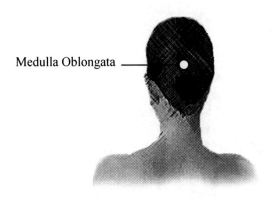

Medulla Oblongata

The other end of the Earth circuit enters approximately 16 to 18 inches into the ground. It is interactive with the pituitary/hypothalamus/pineal complex and attunes the Human electromagnetic field with the crystalline core of the planet. It is this circuit that affects addictions; physical, emotional, mental and psychic. It is within the pituitary/ hypothalamus/pineal complex that the ratio of neuro-transmitters is set.

The Fire Circuit

Fire:
Test point situated on the perineum.

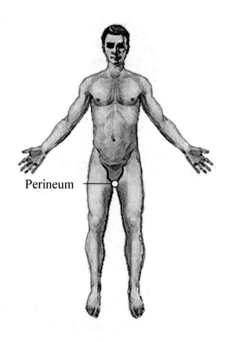

Perineum

To reinstate the Fire circuit is to synthesize the light
and the shadow, and to transcend the life/death/rebirth cycle…
to embrace eternal life.

The Ether Circuits

Heart:
Test point situated over the heart.

Solar:
Test point situated at the solar plexus.

Pubic:
Test point situated at the tip of the pubic bone.

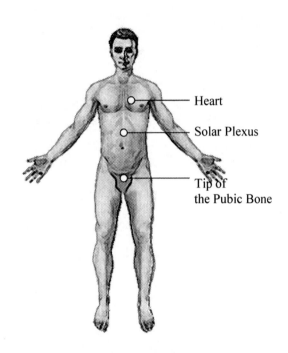

Heart

Solar Plexus

Tip of
the Pubic Bone

The Solar circuit connects us via the Sun to Galactic Center and attunes us to universal identity. Through the knowledge of our global, galactic and universal connection, our sense of individuality is empowered. We feel and understand our function as solar emissaries poised between Earth and stars.

Reconnecting the Heart circuit is to invoke and invite the purity of your soul to represent your Human expression and empower unconditional love to take precedence over all other allegiances and agendas. The Pubic circuit is reconnected by the renunciation of shame, and acknowledging our right to partake of the Tree of Knowledge and the Tree of Life.

Original Innocence Breath Meditation

The following is a transcript of The Template CD recording of the same name.

Your body is a stargate,
a unit of interconnecting, interactive components
whose holonomic, alchemical action creates a sacred space
in which the Mother of Form rises
to meet the Father of Consciousness.

Your body is the pinnacle of the manifest expression
of your spiritual identity.

You are the sensitive instrument of the Benevolence of Creation
whose highest evolutionary purpose
is to become a pure and conscious conduit of light,
to express without censorship the prime impulse of life everlasting
endlessly transmitted by the Heart of the Cosmos.

You are reconnecting through true conscious endeavor
all your visible and invisible energy systems
to reactivate the magnificence of your original blueprint
in order to fully express your Earth instrument.

Water

To embrace forgiveness is to embody the living mandala of love
upon which is based the fundamental Human ethic.

Forgiveness is a forward movement out of judgment and denial.

As you forgive you begin to cooperate with the impeccability
of creation and the evolution of your soul.

As you forgive you shift from victim to creator, shedding
the first layer of mortality ... embracing absolutely
your responsibility for your own life experience.

Life is not happening to you but because of you.
You stand in the center ... generating, orchestrating
and choreographing every movement.

As you breathe these circuits, flood your body, mind and heart
with the compassion that comes from forgiveness.

Understand that all those who you are forgiving
simply needed healing themselves.

Reduce their grief, guilt and pain by sending them your forgiveness.

Gather and release your own grief, anger and guilt,
with your in-breath bringing in understanding, compassion and love,
cleansing your emotional body and creating a matrix
within your electromagnetic field for compassion.

As you experience a deep reunion with mother, father, sisters
and brothers, you are strengthening your ancestral integrity ...
empowering your sense of self by understanding and knowing
that all behavior makes perfect sense.

To forgive is to be forgiven.

Air

As you focus on your Air circuits,
extend your forgiveness
to encompass not only this incarnation
but also all of Human history.

Send your compassion and understanding
down through the ages.

Go beyond the confines of your present identity
to embrace all the dark power holders that have for all time
instilled fear within Human consciousness.

Extend to them your forgiveness.

Understand that they have given your soul growth ...
they have initiated you into the shamanic realms
to rise above the chaos

and through the evolution of your consciousness
to synthesize and integrate
the light and the shadow,
to release fear and embrace love.

Breathe in compassion and forgive.

Feel the acceleration of electromagnetic energy and prana
rejuvenate your pineal... see it blossom back to life,
receiving and absorbing the gift of light,
sending that light into every cell of your body.

Release with each breath, fear, breathing in love and compassion.

Relax into your body as it fills with light.

Earth

As you focus on the Earth circuit, know
the other end of this circuit enters 18 inches into the Earth
attuning your electromagnetic field
with the crystalline core of this planet.

As you breathe with this circuit you breathe with your Mother.
This is your Earthly umbilical cord. As you attune with the Earth
you move into the peace of needlessness.

The changes created by the reconnection of the Earth circuit
will take place gradually and harmoniously
as you begin to redefine the way in which you sustain yourself.

Physically you will no longer be able to sustain
your molecular structure by the taking of life in any form
as your matrix is altered through heightened awareness
of your interconnectedness with all creation.

Energy will then be directly assimilated through Sacred Breath
as you internally manufacture in the alchemical laboratory
of your Human body-temple elixirs of life.

This is already happening through the harmonious unfolding
of organic alignments radiating out from your inner core.

As you breathe,
feel every other life form on Earth breathing with you...
there is One Breath...we are all sharing.

Fire

Reconnecting the Fire circuit
confronts death electromagnetically.

The knowledge that
'never was there a time when I did not exist...
never will there come a time when I will cease to be'
is vibrating its frequency cellularly within the arena of the perineum.

Here the acceleration of life-force energy is rejuvenating the gonads,
stimulating them to produce the magical alchemical components
that together create the elixirs of eternal life.

With each breath know ...
you are unborn, eternal, everlasting.

Ether

As you focus on your Solar circuit know that our Sun
is the mediator of intelligence projected as light
from the galactic core to the planetary mind of Earth.

We as biological units of circuitry are the transducers
of this information matrix.

It is in discovering the co-creative nature of our relationship
with the Sun and the Earth that our core identity unfolds within us
and we begin to feel our connection with Source.
As this grand Solar circuit reinstates your resonance with the Source
via the galactic core, you are becoming aware
of those Planetary Evolutionary Guides
who have been with you all your days on this Earth.

As the acceleration of electromagnetic input rejuvenates
your solar plexus, galactic consciousness seeps into your reality.

As you focus on your Heart circuit feel your chest area open
and silently say YES, yes to love.
Relax into the expansion of your heart center
as you invoke unconditional love
to take precedence over all other agendas and allegiances...
know that through love there is no separation...
all is simultaneously one and different...
to love is to be love.

As you breathe with your Pubic circuit know
that the magnificence of your original seeding is a gift
given to you by many sentient sovereign star beings
from many far-flung star systems.

You hold within each cell of your being
that original blueprint that will allow you to explore
any place, time or energy level in the universe.

The wedding of the Mother of Form and the Father of Consciousness
is taking place in your body-temple.
This wedding of God and Goddess within you will be like the dawn,
when the first rays of light penetrate the darkness to touch the clouds
with fiery color and then bend and bow to kiss the tips of trees,
to probe gently the Earthly foliage, penetrating sweetly
the folds of the Goddess garment to reveal and illuminate
the heart of her eternal beauty.

Every leaf and blade of grass responds with ecstatic pleasure
as the Star and Planet are united once again,
the separation of darkness forgotten.
Within every leaf and flower, every insect and blade of grass
a chemical reaction occurs, causing a passionate secretion of energy
that unfolds in waves of ascending currents ...

... a powerful Earth magic born of an elemental brew
of Water, Air, Earth, Fire and Ether
steaming up from the cauldron of creation.

This wedding is now being celebrated in your heart.

*Form
is the
shape of
Consciousness*

Phase II

Activation and Integration

*The 2nd phase within The Template model
is concerned with the activation and integration
of the first 12 circuits reconnected in
The Ceremony of Original Innocence,
and the reanimation of the geometric Soul Covenant
embedded in the Human matrix.*

There are, within this phase, 2 Ceremonies:

The 13th Circuit Ceremony
and
The Sacred Breath Ceremony

*Sacred Geometric
forms transmit the higher
creation frequencies
that resonate with
our original blueprint,
prior to genetic modification
of the Human DNA*

The Sacred Geometry of The Template

**Conscious communion with Sacred Geometry
is a fundamental aspect of our evolutionary wakening.**

*In seeking illumination on the higher physics of creation,
in order to understand the mechanisms that govern the implicate
order of all manifest existence and to realize the full Human
potential within this whole system of holonomic evolution,
we find ourselves in the realm of Sacred Geometry.*

*The Human DNA code, like all else in the living universe,
is built upon hyper-cooperative, interactive energy pathways
of ultra-organized, creative intelligence.
This creation code is the intelligent patterning of information
that spells out the gift of creation specific to the complete
Human blueprint. The various octaves that make up this harmonic
code have been donated by many sentient sovereign beings
from many far-flung star systems that gave of their genetics
in a time of peace that was sealed with the symbol of the BIRD.*

*Embedded in the Human matrix - out of reach of any form
of manipulation - the Covenant that is the soul blueprint
is written in the Sacred Geometric language of light.
The primary infrastructure of all existence is light ...
all is light ... all is geometry.*

*As Sacred Geometry is a configurative language of the elemental
components of the divine creative force that gives birth to all life,
it offers a direct conduit to Prime Consciousness... to Source,
bypassing the dogmatic perimeters of the intellect to transmit
knowledge that exists beyond the reach of religion, philosophy,
belief or disbelief. Sacred Geometry is pure language
that cares not for the country you come from,
the color of your skin or your cultural beliefs.
It seeks only to unify humanity by exposing the interrelating
harmony that lies at the heart of our creation.*

***As we interact with Sacred Geometric forms, we are communing
with the higher creation frequencies that resonate with our original
blueprint… prior to genetic modification of the Human DNA.***

*One of the most important discoveries of the new quantum
physics is that of the holographic nature of the universe.
Each Human is a fractal aspect of the universal holography.
The geometric language of light, that forms the underlying
matrix of this hologram, is the alphabet of the new paradigm.
Although due to its genetic modification, the present manifestation
of the Human race is not representing the full potency
of that hologram, the blueprint for this immortal template exists
within the Soul Covenant embedded in the Human matrix.
As we commune with Sacred Geometric forms we interact with their
fields of informational influence. Their energetic radiance emits
a frequency that communes with the vibratory infrastructure of our
original blueprint in search of a like frequency with which to resonate.
Through this resonant feedback, the structural integrity of the original
Human template, present in the Soul Covenant, is reinforced.*

*When a specific design and progression of these geometric
creation codes are ceremoniously united with a consciously
spoken resonant sonic code, an alchemy is created that triggers
coherence between the vibratory infrastructure
of the Soul Covenant and the incarnate physical body.
This coherence follows pathways of electromagnetic circuitry.*

*In order to understand the implicate order of our own creation
we need to expose ourselves to the luminous simplicity of the language
in which it is written – the Sacred Geometric language of light.
The Sacred Geometric configuration of the 6 elemental alchemical
components of creation (Water, Air, Earth, Fire, Ether and Stellar
Radiance) in their 3 stages of manifestation (Iconic, Embryonic
and Crystallization), are the components within the alchemical code
of The Template Ceremonies. The resonant transmission
of these forms, in their various creation formulae, replicates
the Soul Covenant embedded in the Human matrix.
(See ' Resurrecting the Geometric Soul Covenant')*

The Language of Light
The Sacred Wedding

*When meditating on the Sun just before sunset, it is possible
to differentiate the beams of light that pulsate so miraculously
from this grand Star as liquid gold fractal transmissions,
an unremitting endless code of light intelligence. This light code,
a cascade of radiant matrices, holds the evolutionary harmonic
that merges with the magnetic Gaia rhythms pulsating
out from the Earth's bio-spheric aura.*

*The embrace of these two potencies of creation
is the sacred marriage of the Mother of Form and the Father
of Consciousness, the quantum Tantra of creation.*

All of the natural world is born of this union.

*Nature is a series of codes and counter resonances,
building, between the two, a matrix of archetypal patterning
that translates this quantum Tantric relationship into the principles
of matter, expressing this alchemical union as life forms that walk,
fly and swim; clothed in fur, feather and skin, trees, flowers
and shimmering wings, all sprung from a palette of light.*

*These codes are written in the language
of light geometry... Sacred Geometry.*

The Creation Waveforms
of Electricity and Magnetism

*As one of the two waveforms of creation,
light is the radiant primal life impulse endlessly transmitted
from the Galactic Directive and translated by our Sun.
Light holds within it codes which reach out to our Earth
for resonant fields with which to create.*

*The transmission of the electric information data that is light
remains a stream of non-manifest potency until it unifies
with a magnetic, gravitational resonant field.
It is the magnetic potency of Earth's gravitational field which,
spiraling up from her bio-spheric aura, provides this field
- the unified field of manifest existence.*

*The egg-like feminine receptors of the magnetic Earth pulse
provide the integrity of form, taking the electric light
directive of the seed impulse through integration
and synthesis into crystallization.*

*Through the embrace of these two concentric waveforms
of creation is conceived the hologram of manifest existence.
The 13th Circuit Ceremony of Activation and Integration,
through its design and progression, creates a field
of resonance for this creation code, drawing you
into the courtship of creation and building a conduit
of coherent conscious communion between your incarnate
body presence, your original blueprint and,
ultimately, the Source of your creation.*

The 13th Circuit
- Activation and Integration
The Physics of Consciousness and the Archetypal Arena

*The reconnection of the 13th Circuit of Activation and Integration
is the first introduction to the full spectrum of the 3rd dimensional
frequency. This frequency is translated in the Human energy field
as a result of communion with the influential harmonic
transmitted by the design and progression of 23 forms
of geometric fractals of 3rd dimensional creation code
in unison with their sonic counterparts.*

*This Ceremony activates the 'occipital terminus' of the 13th Circuit
to function as a delivery system and decoder of the 3rd dimensional
creation code. The function of the 'coccyx terminus'
of the 13th Circuit is to integrate this code into the time/space
co-ordinates of the incarnate body presence.
The reconnection of this circuit of electromagnetic intelligence
is a major step in the re-synthesis of the Human energy field
into the governing mechanism of the universal holography,
bypassing the sentimental, fear, shame and guilt-based
programming of historical orthodox religions
that are tearing the world apart.*

*This influx of intelligence data, originating from the Source
of the hologram, impacts the Human at the level of the core
identity and begins the cleansing of the archetypal arena
by redefining the meaning of Source/God directly,
through the energetic language of creation.
The erroneous definition of Source/God is the most malevolent
and powerful manipulation of consciousness.
This quintessential mycelium of deception has been perpetrated
in a myriad of ways, including the manipulation
of historic recall and the insertion of a false ancestry.*

*This false inheritance has entrenched within the psyche
the archetypal duality of the demonic and angelic models,
creating conflict on the deepest strata of Human behavioral
reference and resulting in deep wounds of separation,
spiritual abandonment and betrayal.*

*In order to realize and stabilize the new paradigm
that will spring from the redefinition of Source, we must establish,
within the archetypal arena, the iconic model that defines
our highest evolutionary purpose: to function as conduits
and instruments of light and love.
This is the prime function of the Ceremony of Activation
and Integration that reconnects the 13th Circuit.*

*This Ceremony is a replica of the courtship of creation, holding
the frequency model of the **activating** life-directive transmitted
from the Heart of the Cosmos and the receptive **integrating** pulse
that emanates from the crystalline core of this planet Earth, placing
the individual unit of circuitry as the conjugal mediator of these two
creation frequencies, resurrecting the Human body-temple
as the sacred enclosure for the sacred wedding
of the Mother of Form and the Father of Consciousness.*

*This Ceremony bypasses the present model of historical and cultural
behavior (and the patriarchally prejudiced language that it employs)
to transcend the dualistic framework of present day psychology and
psychiatry and escort you into the arena of alchemical experience
which allows for the healing of the deep wounds of abandonment and
betrayal that have dogged the Human race. This occurs not through
intellectual analysis but by reconnecting the Human electromagnetic
field energetically to the magnitude of the life impulse emanating
endlessly from the Galactic Core and by enticing Human
consciousness through the gateway of life eternal, linking
its spiraling energy field into the electromagnetic wheels
of the never-beginning, never-ending cycle of existence,
radiating from the Monadic, omnipotent,
omnipresent Source Awareness.*

*The embrace of this holonomic model that governs all of existence
resurrects the potential for self-rejuvenation that is our natural state.
We are an immortal race locked into a mortal realm.*

*The 13th Circuit Ceremony of Activation and Integration brings
electromagnetically the vibrational liberation
from this dimensional prison.*

*The immortal core identity rises phoenix-like
from the Soul Covenant to embrace the divine matrix of form
that is the physical body.*

*Consciousness awakes within the fulcrum point of manifest
creation within the unified field. The 'victim' becomes
the creation and the creator.*

You are not only this, you are the universe.

The 13th Circuit Ceremony

"Deep within the cell a holographic memory
Programmed simultaneous universal history
Pulsing through the system towards a new reality
Dancing through the veins of all Humanity"
From "You, The Masterpiece" by Jiva Carter

The 13th Circuit Ceremony initiates the cleansing of the archetypal
arena not by reprogramming it but by attuning the heart/body/mind
system to the resonance of the geometric Soul Covenant embedded
in the Human matrix that is the original Human blueprint.
The design and progression of the 23 geometric fractals
of the 3 dimensional creation code and their sonic counterparts
are resonant with the various aspects of the holonomic agreement
that lies at the heart of the Human masterpiece.
As this agreement is awakened through frequency resonance,
the 13th Circuit is reinstated. The sonic code is an alchemical
component within this resurrection that linguistically redefines
the Human as a sentient sovereign entity, able to access and translate
the full spectrum of the life-directive present in the informational
matrix of light. This reinforces the primal resonant integrity
of the Human celestial seeding and the soul's lineage present within
the evolutionary harmonic 'seed codes' that are the Tree of Life
and the Tree of Knowledge, a creation code given by many
sentient beings from many different star systems.

Each of the 23 pieces of Sacred Geometry corresponds to an aspect
of the 'holonomic symbiotic code' of the Covenant, in which
the Human design is the sensory organ for planetary transcendence,
and Earth (and the entire solar system) is the counter resonant
organ for Human transcendence. This harmonic galactic identity
is evident within the stunning sonic code that begins by honoring
our connection to "the reservoir of pleasure and causal desire"
and continues on with the many facets of the quintessential
divine identity that defines the Human as an instrument
of light and love for the Benevolence of Creation.

The Pranic Causeway

The reconnection of both terminals of the 13th Circuit in the occiput and coccyx opens and prepares the "pranic causeway" that forms a tubular capsule around the spinal column. Mapped throughout this causeway are ultra sensitive nodal receptors that represent the entire endocrine system. Each receptor is resonantly programmed to identify a fractal of the bio-informational creation signal present in the atomic structure of prana. Each node has a geometric resonant receptor that corresponds to a twin resonance within the structure of the pranic signal. This signal is a life-directive emanating from the Benevolent Source of Creation and holds the immortal code.

As the node receives the signal, it is then transmitted to the relevant endocrine organ. The more capable the receptors are of receiving the full spectrum of the pranic code, the more bio-informational life resonance is transmitted to the endocrine system and the more of the Tantric language of light present in prana is available for translation, utilization and transmittance by the full spectrum of the Human heart/body/mind complex. This capability is activated and integrated in The Sacred Breath Ceremony as 7 circuits in the pranic mechanism are reconnected. This is further investigated in "The Sacred Breath Ceremony" section of this book.

*I acknowledge and honour
my physical being
as the pinnacle
of manifestation
of my spiritual identity*

Resurrecting
the Geometric Soul Covenant
The physical body is as sacred as the soul.

*In the teachings of orthodox religions, the soul is always immortal
and far superior to the flesh and bones of the body. The same
dualistic perception of separation defines heaven as 'up there'
and hell in the center of the Earth. It is this focus upon the spirit,
the soul, the unseen, as more worthy of our respect than the
incarnate, disposable fabric of material existence that allows
for the abuse of our bodies and the desecration of our environment.
The separation of spirit from matter is the founding reference,
originating from the iconic model within the psyche,
that leads both to our estrangement from the governing
mechanism that would gift us with the immortal continuum,
and to the present neuro-psycho-biology that initiates
the deterioration of the physical body into death.*

*Everything about the Ceremonies of Activation and Integration
is focused towards the reunification of spirit and matter,
of body and soul.*

*The linguistic code and the visual synthesis of geometric
configurations echo and mirror the integration, synthesis
and crystallization of these two potencies of creation.
The linguistic code that accompanies the Tantric Star
(Star Tetrahedron) acknowledges the body as the sacred
enclosure for the sacred marriage of spirit and matter.*

*Each Ceremony within The Template series
ends with these words:*

*"I acknowledge and honor my physical being
as the pinnacle of manifestation of my spiritual identity."*

*This is a powerful and healing statement that echoes
the frequency of physical immortality as it recognizes
the sacred Tantric union of spirit and matter.*

The soul cannot be 'found' within the genetic material from which we are constructed. It is, however, the energetic inspiration that allows for manifestation of this material - the blueprint for the blueprint. The genetic code within the DNA is the 'read out' of the extent to which the entity is embodying the Soul Covenant.

The soul is an inter-dimensional hyper-fractal and exists within every molecule of your being. What you see of your 'self' in the mirror is that fractal of your Soul Covenant that has made it across the bridge - the portion that has been birthed into form, the blueprint of your Soul Covenant activated and integrated by your ability to translate the language it is written in - light - the fraction of the creation code that you are able to download into manifest existence and which the morphogenetic field is able to support and quantify.

This fractal of your identity is being dictated by the genetic modification of your DNA and the disconnection of your circuitry.

When you begin to think in terms of holograms you see that nothing exists in isolation. Everything is a part of everything else.

The Soul Covenant, rather than a sentimentalized lofty censoring device that registers all your shameful 'sins', is instead a living schematic of information that requires your ability to access it and birth it into physical being.

Our thoughts and actions that move in opposition to the Covenant - in which 'to give and receive love in all that we do' is the foundation requirement - closes the heart center and retards the soul's expression in our bodies, our lives, our world.

The original Human blueprint is a fractal of the hyper-holographic universe.

*Your blood contains the same divine essence and molecular
alchemy as the rivers that run to the sea, your bones made
of the same elemental components as the ancient stone monoliths
that have silently witnessed the passing of eons.
We are continually exchanging a dataflow of Source Intelligence
with the body of Earth and every form of life within Her embrace,
as circuits of electromagnetic exchange bind us together
as one living ocean of psycho-sensory, interconnected
space/time co-ordinates within the universal order.*

*Never was there a 'time' when any form of life within this ocean
did not exist, as all of life transits within this field of existence
to recreate itself in whatever form is available within the matrix,
taking into the next incarnation the data it has gathered,
repeating the cycle until it learns to break the cycle of degeneration
by breaking the codes of creation. When a critical mass of gathered
Source Intelligence is transmitted from a consciously awakened
group of individuals within this field and fed into the bio-spheric
membrane of the morphogenetic grid, the present paradigm
explodes with light, no longer able to hold back the tides
of the unborn, eternal, everlasting continuum.*

*As we expand and mutate into light-translating units of bio-circuitry
within this whole mechanism, we open portals into the symbiosis
of the Soul Covenant that allow for the growth and evolution of our
solar system, our galaxy and our universe to seep into our everyday
domesticity, to transform the mundane into the transcendent,
bursting the seams of superficiality that masquerade as culture
to allow the radiant emissaries of light to delineate
a new model of existence, beyond the present pain
of being Human, beyond fear.*

**All this evolutionary potential is already in our keeping,
within our Soul Covenant, and within our bodies.**

The Geometric Soul Covenant
and the Ceremonies of Activation and Integration

*Like all else in the living universe, the Soul Covenant embedded
in the Human matrix is built upon the vibratory infrastructure
of a mycelium of energy pathways that are geometric. The particular
creation code of the Human Soul Covenant holds a spatial cognizance
that is not only in holonomic resonance with Earth's 'Gaia-spheric
receptor-codes' but also holds an evolutionary resonance
with the directive intelligence codes of Stellar Radiance emanating
from every celestial body in the solar system and every subsystem
of every galaxy and every universe thereafter.*

*All existence performs upon the mechanics of holography
- an interspatial, inter-dimensional Celtic knot-work
of electromagnetic information systems, embracing all
- from the subatomic to the multi-universal.*

*The data bank of the Soul Covenant is not a fixed linear consequential
readout of information that runs on a time line, but rather a living
vibrating 'torus' of inter-dimensional, interactive, interconnecting,
co-creative holonomic systems; systems that share spatial cognizance,
a self-inventing Rubik Cube of interlacing mandalic codes,
a holographic vehicle through which any time or energy level
in the universe can be experienced. This holographic vehicle
has been known in various ancient texts as the Mer-Ka-Ba;
of which the Star Tetrahedron is a fractal.*

*This Mer-Ka-Ba is the Geometric Soul Covenant,
holographically embedded in the Human matrix,
and holds the blueprint for the original Human design
prior to genetic modification.*

*This blueprint is written in the geometric language of light.
The holography of this blueprint is a symbiotic code in which
the Human design is the sensory organ for planetary ascension
as Earth is the sensory organ for Human ascension.*

The geometric directive/receptive transmissions of electricity and magnetism are transduced and translated through the Human body/presence and simultaneously/holonomically form the 'virtual semblance' of the body/instrument, manifesting through the activation and integration of the geometric Soul Covenant embedded within the Human matrix.

The Soul Covenant is the original Human template prior to genetic modification. It is that which defines us as universal progenitors of life - able to create. This is the quintessence of our divine nature and the way in which we mirror the creation code that lies at the heart of the cosmic hyper-hologram.

As has been said, the higher physics of creation are a system of codes and counter resonances - The Template Ceremonies are a replica of this creation code present in the Soul Covenant. The reconnection of circuitry is the result of the counter resonance experienced by the Human electromagnetic field in response to the code.

The alchemical Ceremonies that lie at the core of "The Template - A Holonomic Model of Transcendence" form a resonant counterpart for the Soul Covenant. The sole purpose of The Template Ceremonies is to resurrect the blueprint...the light body.

In The 13th Circuit Ceremony, the Sacred Geometric language of light is objectified through the visual embrace of this language by the actual presence of the geometry. Together with the resonant linguistic code that replicates this fractal of the Soul Covenant, the 13th Circuit is reinstated.

The geometric language of light is configured in the full spectrum of the 3rd dimension. As the 13th Circuit is reconnected via resonance with this language, the full electromagnetic frequency of the 3rd dimension is introduced to the Human energy field.

We have not yet entered the full manifestation of the 3rd dimension.

The 3rd Dimension
Fully Manifest in Form

*Contrary to popular belief, the full manifestation of the 3rd dimension
is the highest evolutionary challenge for the Human race at this time,
not only because, in its full glory, it is a realm of beauty beyond
the imagination of the most talented visionary artist but because
it is the stargate to all other dimensions.*

*On Earth in this time zone, we are experiencing the lower octave
of the 3rd dimension called 'duality'. It is a frequency zone mutually
created by the oscillating transmissions of several billion-brainwave
patterns and their environmental visual/audible feedback, as 'reality'
validates the mutant state of the Human DNA through war, famine,
genocide and the subjugation of the natural world.*

*These wave patterns are emanating from a central complex
in the Human brain and are the bio-informational signals transmitted
by the ratio of neuro-chemicals manufactured and stabilized
in this alchemical crucible. The atomic compositions and ratios
of these chemicals are determined by the function and interaction
of the 3 magical glands: the pituitary, hypothalamus and pineal.
These glands are in atrophy, as is the entire endocrine system,
as a result of the disconnection of the circuitry that provides them
with their electromagnetic life-force.*

*The atomic make-up of the neuro-chemicals produced by these glands
is ultimately geometric. The incompetent ratio of these chemicals,
due to the atrophy of the manufacturing organ, results
in the dormancy of several configurations of the geometric
spectrum of the 3rd dimensional life-directive. This is mirrored
not only in the behavioral modification of the Human race
but also in the natural world. The fractal composition that dictates
the dimensional expression of nature is missing parts
of the holographic prism through which light is photo-synthesized,
and so expresses a lesser vibrancy and spectrum of color.*

"In the full manifestation of 3rd dimensionality, coexisting with all other prime dimensions, there are trees so deeply green they are almost as blue as midnight. Each leaf is as a facetted jewel that when slightly turned emanates a fractal beam of deep violet with a golden hue shining out from its core... and suddenly there for a moment is the most brilliant opal-hued silver flash! Water...water... liquid crystal... lavender beams swimming in its depths... becoming pink and palest blue and creamy opal-white; and geometry dancing beneath it all as every living thing celebrates together the conscious ceremony of life eternal for here there is no shadow... no separation. So much light, as the grand Maha-spheric Sun embraces you with each beam of light ... a thousand loving arms, a cosmic embrace. And when it sinks away into the turquoise indigo night of a billion stars you will not sleep but awaken into a realm of celestial dreaming; listening within the cathedral night to the starry orchestra, starchild that you are, riding on the alpha wave of deep inner star-studded space to the shores of morning light. And there again, the Sun that never left but only withdrew that you might know it through its starry consorts, returns now as dawn's caress upon this beloved Earth, as Sunrise brings the promise of another day filled only with the joy of living...and loving."

From a work in progress by Juliet Carter

This dimension exists now, here on Earth and within us.

Our collective consciousness has chosen to focus within this frequency zone because this is where it is needed, to resurrect our ability to receive, translate and transmit the full spectrum of the radiance matrix of the creation directive: light.

As a seed race we are coded to respond to various cultural and environmental stimuli to awaken from the dream of duality. As we throw off the sleep of ages, connecting back into the never ending or beginning slipstream of universal dataflow, each of us becomes a portal, a worldbridger. As we collectively amass a global resonant field of Source Awareness through resurrected circuitry, we stabilize a bridge for the exodus of our immortal race, to return to its rightful place within the Galactic holography - within the immortal continuum -

for those who so choose.

*We will then begin the journey of conscious development that has been
arrested by the modification of our DNA, the disconnection
of our circuitry and by the destabilization of our solar system which
has aborted us from the womb of holistic evolution - an evolution
not defined by the acceleration of technology, or the discovery
of cures for the ever-escalating number of plagues, while our
children continue to be abused, and while most of the world
lives in abject misery, poverty and fear; this is not evolution!
This is simply a mutant detour to render our prisons more
comfortable for those who can afford it.*

*As illumination reaches some, the darkness escalates.
Such is the genius of this dualistic paradigm, containing as it does
its own self-regulating system of wardenship. To break out
of this frequency zone we must cooperate and unify our intentions,
coming out of denial of the global situation and understanding
that it is not enough to make this reality work for you personally
by seeing all your ever-expanding comfort zones satiated
through a hollow definition of 'abundance'.*

*Evolution will begin with the reconnection to Source
and the autonomous definition of that Source within the Human psyche,
beyond the imposition of those who have written the history books
through the prism of their own desires and agendas.*

*As the fetus of Humankind once again draws succor
from its umbilical connection to the Benevolent Heart of Creation,
Source Consciousness awakens to us, within us,
seeding the embryogenesis that will birth
the Transcendental Human.*

*The stargate of the 3rd dimension beckons to us...
step through the portal ceremoniously...
it is so easy...it has already happened.*

*Feel the deep magnetic pull of the universal hologram
drawing you into the eye of the joyous storm of life eternal.*

It will not fail you ... its power is love.

*The reconnection
of circuitry
is fundamental
to the transmutation
of the life/death/rebirth
cycle*

Sacred Geometry

Sacred Geometry is the 'graphic code' that reveals the processes of inherent order underlying all of creation.

*The mathematical laws of Sacred Geometry govern
every system of growth, every motion in the universe,
from atomic bonds to spiraling galaxies.
As these geometric laws coalesce from the sphere, they map,
through a language of relationship, the consciousness
of creation with number, angle, shape, and form.*

*Throughout the centuries in many cultures around the planet,
Sacred Geometry has been used in architecture and art
with the intention of harmonizing with the principles of regeneration
coded into the pure mathematics that are the resonant counterpart
between the Human template and creative force.*

*The often used mathematical law to which both ancient
and modern artists and architects have looked for inspiration
is the **Golden Mean** or **Golden Ratio**. As revealed throughout
the natural world, it beckons us to recognize the pattern
of creation and regeneration.*

*There are a myriad of geometric shapes, combinations,
and permutations.*

*In the following pages are the geometric configurations relevant to
The Ceremony of Activation and Integration, The 13th Circuit.*

The Golden Mean
- Phi 1.618 Φ

What do we mean by "mean" when we say Golden Mean?

The term "mean" identifies the relationship of a number
as the middle point of two extremes.

Arithmetic "means" are equal

So 4 is the **arithmetic** mean of 2 and 6 because 4 is equally distant between
the two in **addition**: $2 + 2 = 4$ and $4 + 2 = 6$

$$0 \quad 1 \quad 2 \quad 3 \quad 4 \quad 5 \quad 6 \quad 7 \quad 8$$

Geometric "means" have a common multiplier

For example, the geometric mean of 2 and 8 is 4, because the relationship
of 4 to 2 and 8 is that of equal distance between the two by **multiplication:**

$$2 \times 2 = 4 \quad \text{and} \quad 4 \times 2 = 8$$

$$0 \quad 1 \quad 2 \quad 3 \quad 4 \quad 5 \quad 6 \quad 7 \quad 8$$

The Golden Mean

The Golden Mean is a specific geometric mean with an additional rule.

In the previous geometric mean, $2 \times 2 = 4$ and $4 \times 2 = 8$, but $2 + 4 = 6$, not 8.
The Golden Mean imposes the additional requirement that the two segments
that define the mean also add to the length of the entire line segment:

$$0 \quad 1 \quad 2 \quad 3 \quad 4 \quad 5 \quad 6 \quad 7 \quad 8$$

This only occurs at one point. You can see in the illustration above that it is
just a little less than 5/8ths, or 0.625, or to be more precise, 0.6180339887...
calculated into infinity..., where:

A is to B as B is to C and B + C = A

An Infinite Question and the Spiraling Path of Regeneration

Like **pi**, the numerical value of **phi** is infinitely indefinable as, at the linear level, there has never been found a recurring pattern in the infinitely expanding numbers to the right of the decimal.

Below are some visual aids to see the **Φ** in action:

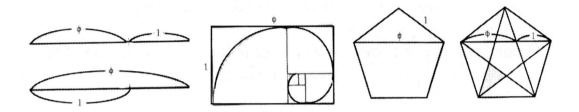

This principle is mirrored throughout the structures of the body.

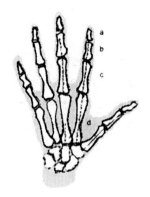

For example, the length of each bone segment in our fingers is in proportionate ratio to the adjoining segment by approximately

1 to 1.618

[d = c x 1.618]   [c = b x 1.618]   [b = a x 1.618]

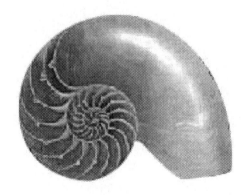

Within its spiral formation, the nautilus reveals the Golden Ratio.

Each chamber has progressively 1.618 times more volume than the preceding chamber.

The Fibonacci Series

Another pattern of interest is the Fibonacci series, which is found throughout nature and is closely related to **phi**.

In the 12th century, Leonardo Fibonacci discovered a numerical series that holds a mathematical relationship behind **phi**.

Starting with 0 and 1, each new number in the series is the sum of the two before it.

0, 1, 1, 2, 3, 5, 8, 13, 21, 34, 55, 89, 144, . . .

The ratio of each successive pair of numbers in the series approximates **phi** (1.618)

For example, 5 divided by 3 is 1.666 ..., 8 divided by 5 is 1.60.

The table following shows how the ratios of the successive numbers in the Fibonacci series converge on **phi** or Φ. By the 10th number every successive sum rounds off to 1.618 and after the 40th number in the series, the ratio is 1.618033988749895 which is accurate to15 decimal places.

The ratio of successive Fibonacci numbers converges on **phi**

Sequence in the series	Resulting Fibonacci number (the sum of the two numbers before it)	Ratio of each number to the one before it (this estimates **phi** or Φ)
0	0	
1	1	
2	1	1.000000000000000
3	2	2.000000000000000
4	3	1.500000000000000
5	5	1.666666666666667
6	8	1.600000000000000
7	13	1.625000000000000
8	21	1.615384615384615
9	34	1.619047619047619
10	55	1.617647058823529
11	89	1.618181818181818
12	144	1.617977528089888
13	233	1.618055555555556
37	24,157,817	1.618033988749897
38	39,088,169	1.618033988749894
39	63,245,986	1.618033988749895
40	102,334,155	1.618033988749895

Zero - Fifth Dimension

ZerO Dimension
The Infinitesimal

What's the Point?

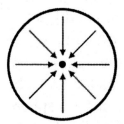

All geometry begins with a point. This point is considered zero point, the infinitesimal [infinitely dividable] reference point. This point, eternally vanishing into nothingness equally from all sides is, therefore, eternally a sphere.

The numerical 0 is a circle, a 2-dimensional symbol of the sphere. It is a border around a hole, a fractal unit of the whole, empirically symbolizing the beginning and the end, or nothing. The 0 revolutionized the system of calculation and the negative numbers; -1 -2 etc. placed 0 as the middle point.

Infinity includes the infinitesimal

Normally we think of infinity as beginning from a point, the Earth, ourselves, etc. and extending out in all directions infinitely. To truly understand infinity we must realize that it is also extending inward from every direction infinitely. Every reference point is the gateway between the **"infinite in"** and the **"infinite out"**. Geometry begins, therefore, with geometry! However abstractly we try to conceptualize the infinitesimal, a 3-dimensional sphere will always be a fractal of the whole.

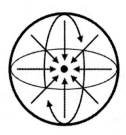

1st Dimension

Whose line is it anyway?

Taking the infinitesimal point and extending it, we create a line
- the shortest path between two points. We call this line the 1st dimension.
Conceptually, like the point, it is infinitely thin. However, it has created
differentiation between point (a) and point (b), between above and below,
left and right - it has begun the definition of duality. Regardless of how
thin we conceive it to be, it has a top and a bottom and so, therefore, it also
contains a plane. Since the point is a sphere, the line (an extended point)
is a tube - 3-dimensional. But for the sake of utility we will pretend
that it is just a 1-dimensional step to:

2nd Dimension

It's plane to see...

The line, when brought around to join with itself, creates a circle
(here we are back to the 0 again) or a triangle (the least number of points
to join the least number of straight lines back to the origin) and we have
created a plane. We call this plane the 2nd dimension, imagining it
to have only 2 dimensions, length and width. Once again,
(-2) billion microns is still 3D!

Linear and 2-dimensional thinking is where we are generally trapped by
our habitual limited perceptions of reality. This is where we see the surface
of things as their identity, where we linguistically divide everything into
opposites, good and bad, black and white. It is only from this position
that we perceive separation. As we journey from the Monad through
the Dyad, first experiencing separation, we move back through attraction
to reconnect, not to merge back into the One, but to experience,
through the realization of simultaneous individuality and oneness,
the interconnectedness of all. This is the 3rd dimension.

3rd Dimension

Gateway to the Infinite

The 3rd dimension, where the 1st and 2nd dimensions are inseparably experienced as part of the whole, is as much a part of all further delineations as it is of its predecessors. Once we have totally arrived, fully conscious, in the 3rd dimension, we will realize that there is no separation of dimensions and we pass through the gateway into what we have historically identified as multi-dimensionality.

Structure defines relationship. So the 4th dot brings the triangular plane into a tetrahedron, the simplest way to divide equally a sphere - which brings us back to the point.

Taking the point and extending it out equally in all directions, we have a sphere, or on paper a circle. We begin life as a spherical cell on a spherical planet in a spherical universe. Geometry is the study of the whole and our relationships to and with it.

If we take a sphere/circle and move it one half its diameter beside itself, we will produce the symbol of the Vesica Piscis, the archetypal *Yoni* - the means by which we may create all other geometric forms.

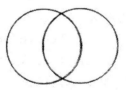

Here, in 2, is the reflection that gives the 1 self-knowledge, and creates a 3rd thing, a relationship, a portal to infinite variety... life. Notice how the relationship of these 2 circles gives us the co-ordinates to create all the shapes needed to form the 5 Platonic and 13 Archimedean 3-dimensional solids.

4th Dimension

An infinity of gateways

Hyper Space

Mathematically, the raising of a number in frequency (ie: the first step would be to square it) is to bring it into the next dimension. Thus a line "squared" becomes a square, then a cube etc.

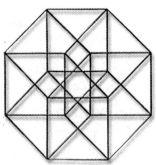

$$2^2 > 2^3 > 2^4 > 2^5$$

As there are an infinite number of planes in any given 3rd dimensional space, similarly there are an infinite number of 3-dimensional co-ordinates in any given 4th dimensional space. A circle is a 2-D representation of the 3-D sphere, so also a cube is a 3-D representation of a hyper cube or 4-D cube. Although all dimensions exist and are eternally inseparable, for the purpose of coming to a deeper understanding from our current perspective, we will view each dimensional step as an expansion of the previous one.

Later in this workbook you will notice that the Platonic solids, the 5 basic classic 3-D shapes, expand to become the 13 Archimedean shapes. These Archimedean forms are 3-D representations of the next order of integration. They are the co-ordinates of the magnetic binding principal in all atomic bonds. These forms, when viewed in this perspective, will begin to reveal "where" we *experience* life.

Dimensions beyond the 3rd will be examined in further depth in Workbook II. I include here only a hint, as it will help to accept our present position in the tapestry of the All. We are not on a journey of escape - leaving the 3rd dimension is not our goal. As we expand our consciousness to become who we already are, we will re - member ourselves, together, as infinite self-reproductive, co-creative unities within the unified field.

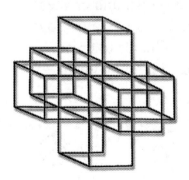

On this page you see 2 versions of a 2-D representation of a hyper-cube. The diagram at the top shows interlocking cubes all expanding out from one central cube.

Here to the left is one cube surrounded by 6 cubes attached to each face, giving the illusion of doubled cube expansion.

5th Dimension

As within, so without

Stellar Radiance

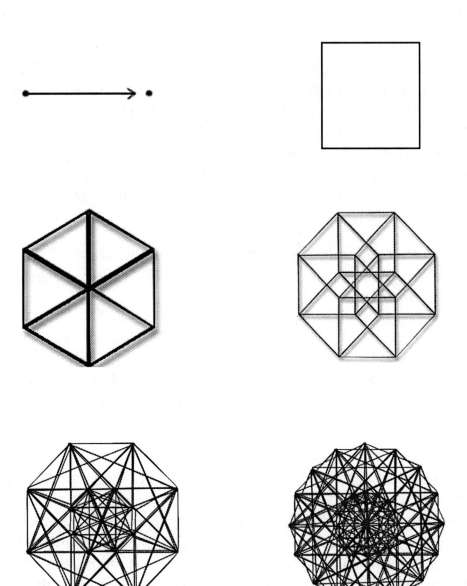

New Paradigm - New Sonic Resonance

As the periphery of the new paradigm begins to permeate our consciousness, the language we use to describe the unfamiliar is mutating. Our new perceptions are bursting the seams of our past understandings and so our language must expand to express these fractals of holographic comprehension.

When we received the sonic code for the reconnection of the 13th Circuit it did not flow in resonance with the currently established names of the corresponding geometric forms. The names did not express the essential qualities of these forms as they related to their function within the Soul Covenant embedded in the Human matrix. Neither did they linguistically recognize the male and female differentiation of Platonic and Archimedean geometry or that they formed the two potencies of the Tantric components within the alchemy of creation.

The information pertaining to the male and female function of Platonic and Archimedean geometry has been given by the Consciousness that is assisting us to assemble The Template.

The spoken code of The 13th Circuit Ceremony is redefining the quintessential Human identity not as the 'Earth orphan', lost in linear space-time, but as the transcendental galactic Human, affirming its symbiotic evolutionary relationship to Earth, the solar system and the entire universal holography.

The orthodox names express these Sacred Geometric forms by explaining their apparent visual and constructive nature but not their esoteric function. They do not touch upon the fact that Sacred Geometry is the language of light, the foundation structure of the new perception of the unified field. Buckminster Fuller had renamed them according to his own expanded perception. Understanding that there is no such thing as a plane, he thought they should not be named according to the number of their planes, i.e. dodecahedron, meaning 12 sides; icosahedron, 20 sides. It was his view that it was the number of connections or vertices that were important and he renamed them accordingly; icosavertexion, dodecavertexion, etc. However, apart from the fact that if there are no planes, there is nothing to connect, Fuller's names were still confined to the arena of mathematics and architecture, and thus did not express the forms as holistic units of consciousness and language.

Shortly after we became aware of all this, the new names arrived.

The components of the names are:

1. The elements: Earth = Terra; Fire = Pyra; Air = Prana; Water = Aqua; Ether = Solar.

2. The indication that each is a division of a sphere. Thus a cube, or hexahedron would become a Terra Sphere.

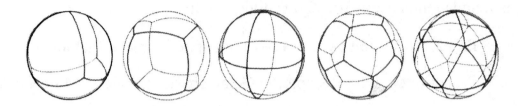

3. The next part of the names came from the recognition of the male and female aspects of the forms:

   a. The Platonic solids are the male Omni Spheres which connect the top of the 13th Circuit and,

   b. The Archimedean solids are the female Gaia Spheres which connect the bottom of the 13th Circuit .

   These include 3 phases as they expand from the basic male Platonic forms to become:

   1. Truncated: Iconic or conceptual,
   2. Rhomboid: Embryonic or synthesis,
   3. Great Rhomboid: Gaia or crystallization.

   Thus a truncated cube in classical Greek terms would be an "Iconic Terra Sphere".

Geometric Tantra

Beyond Duality and into the 3rd Dimension

In the 2nd dimension the Monad reflects itself, becoming the dual counterparts of apparent opposites and creating – through this yin/yang position – the foundations of the 3rd dimension.

This foundation is geometric and is divided into:

a.   Primal Activation Directives - Omni-spheric, male, Platonic

b.   Primal Integrating Receptors - Gaia-spheric, female, Archimedean.

The Ceremonial geometric order is a code, a dance of these male and female forms that is choreographed to the sonic resonance of the Ceremony.

Electric: **Activation** - The resonant test point in the body for the Omni-spheric Activation Code is at the top of the spine in the occiput.

Magnetic: Integration - The resonant test point for the Gaia-spheric Integration Code is at the bottom of the spine in the coccyx.

These 2 points are at the top and the bottom of the 13th Circuit and the pranic causeway that runs concurrent with the spinal column.

The electric seed transmission of the information data that is light, remains a non-manifest transmission until it unifies with a magnetic, gravitational resonant field. Through the embrace of this field is conceived the hologram of manifest existence as the egg-like feminine receptors provide the integrity of form through the integration and synthesis that takes the electric light-directive of the seed impulse through its Iconic and Embryonic stages into Crystallization.

Test points for the 13th Circuit
of Activation and Integration

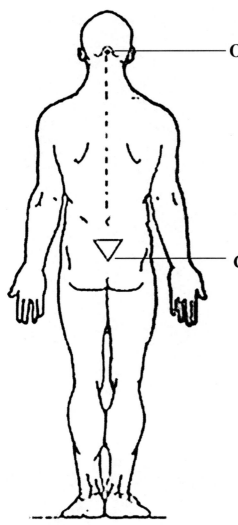

Occiput

Activation -
The resonant test point for the
Omni-spheric Activation Code
is at the top of the spine
in the occiput.

Coccyx

Integration -
The resonant test point for the
Gaia-spheric Integration Code
is at the bottom of the spine
in the coccyx.

136

The Geometry

of

The 13th Circuit
Ceremony

Omni Spheres

Platonic solids

Activation

The 5 Platonic solids and their 3 nestings
used in this Ceremony code.

Aqua

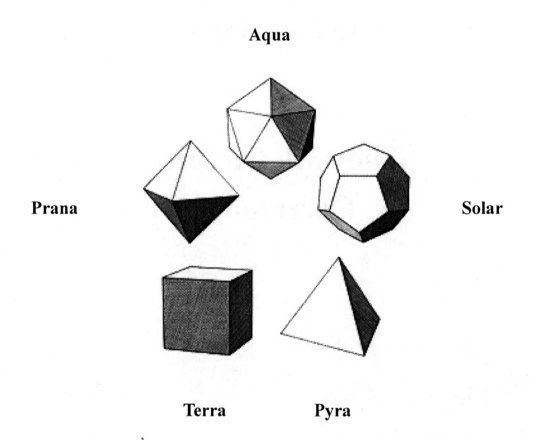

Prana

Solar

Terra

Pyra

Magic Mirrors

Out of many beautiful ways to combine and nest the 5 Omni-spheric geometric structures, there are only three combinations that mirror each other.

First, there is the tetrahedron. Imagine a dot at the center of each face of the tetrahedron. Connect the dots; you then have a tetrahedron inside pointing down. Now expand the smaller tetrahedron in every direction equally until it is the same size as the first one, and you have a star tetrahedron. The tetrahedron is the only Platonic solid that mirrors itself.

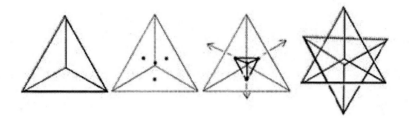

Second, are the cube and the octahedron, which if you follow the same process using either shape you create a mirror of the other.

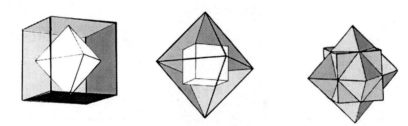

Third, are the icosahedrons and dodecahedrons.

Omni Spheres
Platonic forms

Activation

The 8 Platonic forms are Omni Spheres. They are male, electric and activating: they reconnect the occipital/activation point of the 13th Circuit.

Pyra Sphere	**Tetrahedron**
Tantric Star	**Stellated Octahedron / Star Tetrahedron**
Terra Sphere	**Cube / Hexahedron**
Prana Sphere	**Octahedron**
Terra Prana Sphere	**Cube Octahedron**
Aqua Sphere	**Icosahedron**
Solar Sphere	**Dodecahedron**
Aqua Solar Sphere	**Icosadodecahedron**

Primal Activation Directives

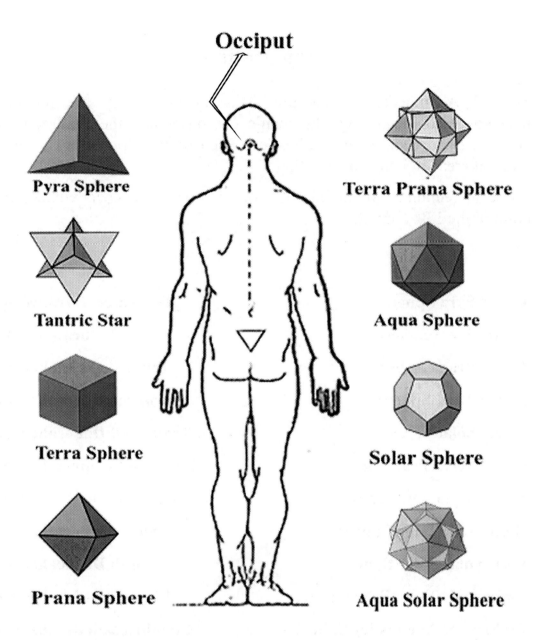

Pyra Sphere

Tantric Star

Terra Sphere

Prana Sphere

Occiput

Terra Prana Sphere

Aqua Sphere

Solar Sphere

Aqua Solar Sphere

Gaia Spheres
Archimedean Forms

Integration

The 13 Archimedean forms are Gaia Spheres. They are feminine, magnetic, and integrating: the Iconic or conceptual, the Embryonic or synthesis, and Gaia, or crystallization. Each progression brings a higher order of creation into manifestation.

These 13 feminine (Archimedean) forms reconnect the coccyx/integration point of the 13th Circuit.

Iconic Pyra Sphere	**Truncated Tetrahedron**
Iconic Terra Sphere	**Truncated Cube**
Iconic Prana Sphere	**Truncated Octahedron**
Iconic Aqua Sphere	**Truncated Icosahedron**
Iconic Solar Sphere	**Truncated Dodecahedron**
Iconic Terra Prana Sphere	**Truncated Cuboctahedron**
Iconic Aqua Solar Sphere	**Truncated Icosadodecahedron**
Embryonic Terra Sphere	**Snub Cuboctahedron**
Embryonic Solar Sphere	**Snub Dodecahedron**
Embryonic Terra Prana Sphere	**Rhombicuboctahedron**
Embryonic Aqua Solar Sphere	**Rhombicosadodecahedron**
Gaia Terra Prana Sphere	**Great Rhombicuboctahedron**
Gaia Aqua Solar Sphere	**Great Rhombicosadodecahedron**

Primal Integrating Receptors

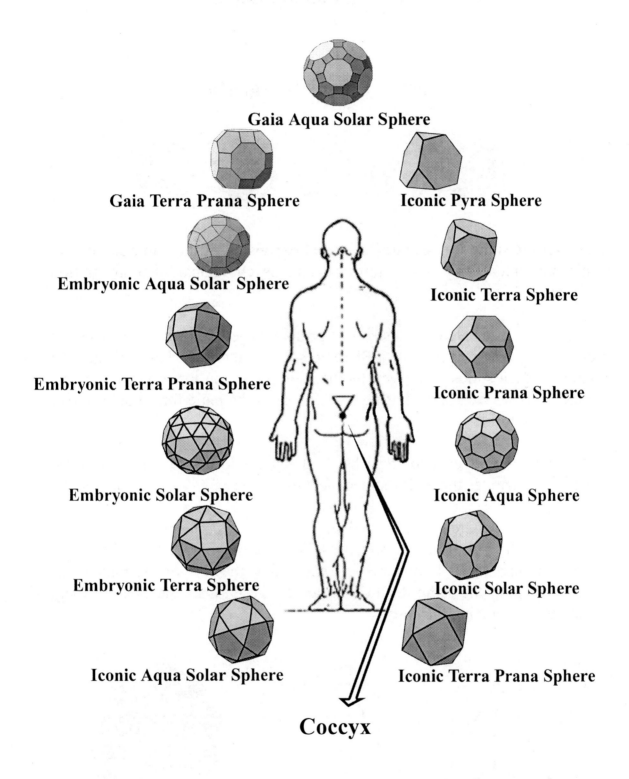

Gaia Aqua Solar Sphere

Gaia Terra Prana Sphere

Iconic Pyra Sphere

Embryonic Aqua Solar Sphere

Iconic Terra Sphere

Embryonic Terra Prana Sphere

Iconic Prana Sphere

Embryonic Solar Sphere

Iconic Aqua Sphere

Embryonic Terra Sphere

Iconic Solar Sphere

Iconic Aqua Solar Sphere

Iconic Terra Prana Sphere

Coccyx

Iconic Spheres
Truncated Platonic Solids

Iconic Forms Integrate

The **Iconic** is the first of three stages of expansion of the feminine. It is at this conceptual stage (both physical and psychological) that integration begins.

The term 'truncated' is used by orthodox geometrists as a way of describing how to get from a Platonic solid to the most basic of the five Archimedean solids. However, the focus is placed on the truncation of the solid. In other words, by cutting something off the male form you arrive at the female form!

However, if you expand the ribs of the male form out until the same distance separates the ends then connect them, the same result is obtained.

For example, where in the normal term 'truncated tetrahedron' the focus is placed on the truncation of the tetrahedron, the diagrams below show how the same end result is obtained by expanding the ribs of the male form outwards until the same distance separates the ends as the ribs are long, and then connecting the ends.

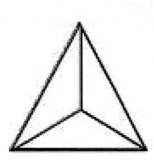  

Dual Element Iconic Spheres

These two Iconic forms are the integrating phase between the mirrored nestings of the Terra Sphere and Prana Sphere:

Iconic Terra Prana Sphere

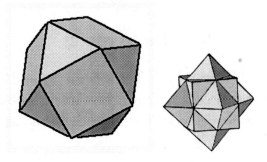

and the Aqua Sphere and Solar Sphere:

Iconic Aqua Solar Sphere

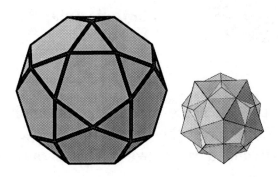

Embryonic Spheres
Rhomboid and Snub

The **Embryonic** is the second stage of the three-phase expansion of the feminine. It is at this embryonic stage that **Synthesis** occurs.

In all these cases Embryonic Spheres are achieved by expanding the faces rather than the edges, as we did with the Iconic Spheres.

Solo Embryonics

The snub in snub cube (Embryonic Terra Sphere) and snub dodecahedron (Embryonic Solar Sphere) comes from the Greek, *cubus simus* - meaning squashed. However, they are more easily understood as expansions.

Embryonic Terra Sphere

Embryonic Solar Sphere

These are the only two elements whose shapes autonomously form the Embryonic stage. Both have the interesting aspect of forming two versions: a left twist and a right twist. This creates a special beauty, balancing symmetry and asymmetry.

Dual Element Embryonic Spheres

The term "rhomboid" is used to describe a sort of explosion of a Platonic solid to form the next two spheres. The first of these is the Embryonic Terra Prana Sphere and is the expansion of both the Terra Sphere/cube and the Prana Sphere/octahedron. The second is the Embryonic Aqua Solar Sphere, which is the expansion of both the Aqua Sphere/icosahedron, and the Solar Sphere/dodecahedron.

 Embryonic Terra Prana Sphere

 Embryonic Aqua Solar Sphere

Gaia Spheres

Gaia is the third of three stages of expansion of the feminine. It is at this stage that **Crystallization** begins. The term "great rhomboid" is used to describe a further expansion of the rhomboid solid to form the next two spheres.

 Gaia Terra Prana Sphere

 **Gaia Aqua Solar Sphere**

The 13th Circuit Geometry

and

Test Points

Each of the following pages shows a photo of the geometry used in The 13th Circuit Ceremony. Most often this is a nesting of two or more individual geometries which are pictured and named to the right of the photo.

The figure below the geometry shows the test points for the circuits affected by this geometry and its combinations.

These are circuits that are connected in the Foundation phase, The Ceremony of Original Innocence. These circuits are further activated and integrated by the reconnection of the 13th Circuit.

The illustrations at the foot of each page show the activation and integration test points and their resonant geometry.

PYRA SPHERE / ICONIC PYRA SPHERE

FIRE

This 1st form in The 13th Circuit Ceremony
is a combination of:

Pyra Sphere

Iconic Pyra Sphere

The circuit of the Foundation Ceremony activated and integrated
by the Pyra Sphere and Iconic Pyra Sphere

This combination of male and female
geometries activates and integrates
the Fire circuit.

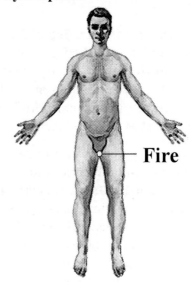

Fire

Test points for the circuit activated and integrated
by the Pyra Sphere and Iconic Pyra Sphere
in The 13th Circuit Ceremony

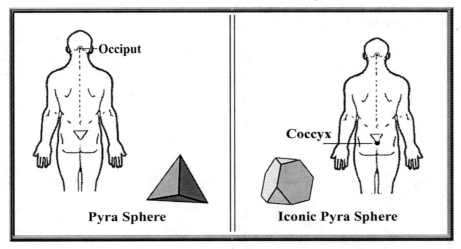

Occiput

Pyra Sphere

Coccyx

Iconic Pyra Sphere

Activates   **Integrates**

TANTRIC STAR

FIRE and AIR

This 2nd form in The 13th Circuit Ceremony is a combination of:

Pyra Sphere

Prana Sphere

The circuits of the Foundation Ceremony activated by the Tantric Star

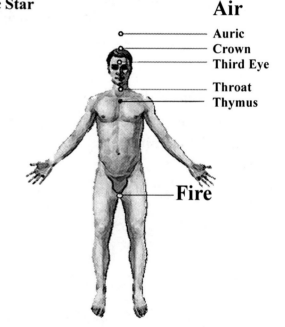

Air
- Auric
- Crown
- Third Eye
- Throat
- Thymus

Fire

The Tantric Star is a nesting of 2 Pyra Spheres (tetrahedrons) interlinked, one pointing up and the other down, automatically creating a Prana Sphere (octahedron) in the center. It is the first of three mirror geometries. The Pyra Sphere is the only one that mirrors itself.

Another way to see it is as 8 Pyra Spheres set like stellations around a Prana Sphere. (This form is sometimes called a stellated octahedron), thus there is the geometric expression of both Air and Fire. Because this form is the Alpha geo-structure in our physical manifestation, it also connects and strengthens the thymus gland, responsible for regulating the immune system.

Test point for the circuits activated by the Tantric Star in The 13th Circuit Ceremony

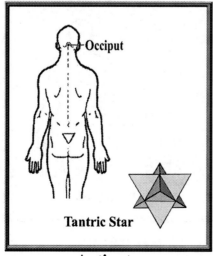

Occiput

Tantric Star

Activates

This picture illustrates the Tantric Star as interlocking Pyra Spheres

This picture illustrates the Tantric Star as a stellated Prana Sphere

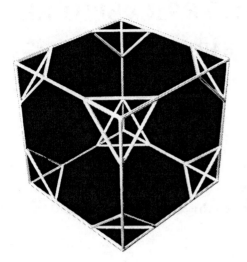

TERRA SPHERE / ICONIC TERRA SPHERE

EARTH

**This 3rd form in The 13th Circuit Ceremony
is a combination of:**

Terra Sphere

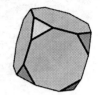

Iconic Terra Sphere

**The circuit of the Foundation Ceremony activated and integrated
by the Terra Sphere and Iconic Terra Sphere**

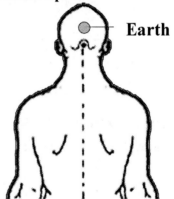

Earth

**This combination of male and female
geometries activates and integrates
the Earth circuit.**

**The Earth circuit test point is the mound in the center of the back of the head just
above the occipital indentation. This circuit runs through the medulla oblongata
and circles 16 - 18 inches into the Earth.**

**Test points for the circuit activated and integrated
by the Terra Sphere and Iconic Terra Sphere
in The 13th Circuit Ceremony**

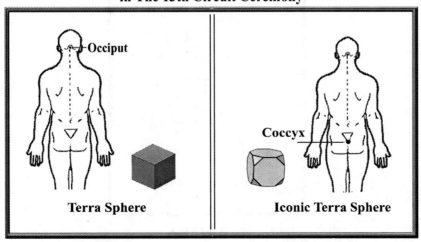

Activates   **Integrates**

EMBRYONIC TERRA SPHERE

EARTH

This 4th form in The 13th Circuit Ceremony is the:

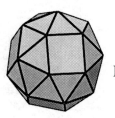

Embryonic Terra Sphere

The circuit of the Foundation Ceremony integrated by the Embryonic Terra Sphere

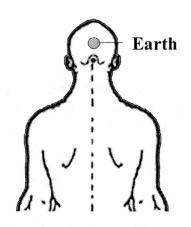

Earth

This female geometric form integrates the Earth circuit.

Test point for the circuit integrated by the Embryonic Terra Sphere in The 13th Circuit Ceremony

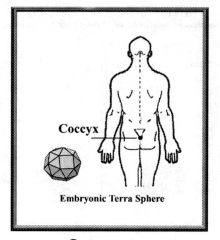

Coccyx

Embryonic Terra Sphere

Integrates

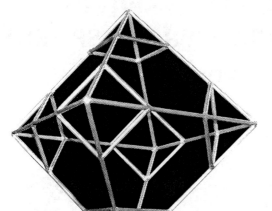

PRANA SPHERE /
ICONIC PRANA SPHERE

AIR

**The 5th form in The 13th Circuit Cermony
is a combination of:**

Prana Sphere   **Iconic Prana Sphere**

**The circuits of the Foundation Ceremony
activated and integrated
by the Prana Sphere and Iconic Prana Sphere**

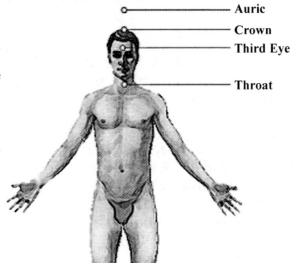

Air
Auric
Crown
Third Eye

Throat

**This combination of male and female
geometries activates and integrates
the Air circuits.**

**Test points for the circuits activated and integrated
by the Prana Sphere and Iconic Prana Sphere
in The 13th Circuit Ceremony**

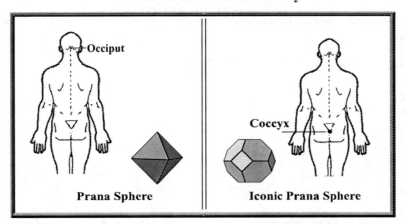

Occiput

Coccyx

Prana Sphere   **Iconic Prana Sphere**

Activates   **Integrates**

155

TERRA PRANA SPHERE / ICONIC TERRA PRANA SPHERE

EARTH and AIR

This 6th form in The 13th Circuit Ceremony is a combination of:

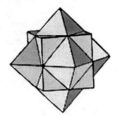

Terra Prana Sphere

Iconic Terra Prana Sphere

**The circuits of the Foundation Ceremony
activated and integrated by the Terra Prana Sphere
and Iconic Terra Prana Sphere**

This combination of male and female geometries activates and integrates the Earth and Air circuits.

The Terra Prana Sphere is the 2nd of the mirrored geometries. In this case the Terra and Prana Spheres mirror each other. The Iconic Terra Prana Sphere is formed as the integrating lines between the two.

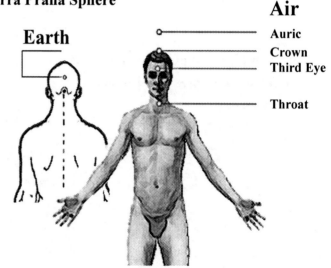

Earth

Air

Auric
Crown
Third Eye

Throat

**Test points for the circuits activated and integrated
by the Terra Prana Sphere and Iconic Terra Prana Sphere
in The 13th Circuit Ceremony**

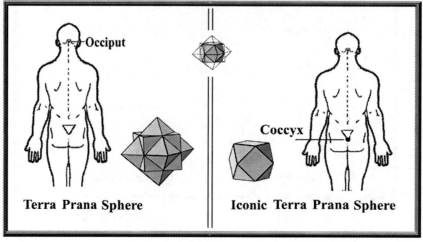

Occiput

Coccyx

Terra Prana Sphere

Iconic Terra Prana Sphere

Activates

Integrates

156

EMBRYONIC TERRA PRANA SPHERE / GAIA TERRA PRANA SPHERE

EARTH and AIR

This 7th form in The 13th Circuit Ceremony is a combination of:

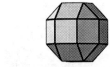

Embryonic Terra Prana
Sphere

Gaia Terra Prana
Sphere

The circuits of the Foundation Ceremony integrated
by the Embryonic Terra Prana Sphere and Gaia Terra Prana Sphere

This combination of female
geometries integrates the
Earth and Air Circuits.

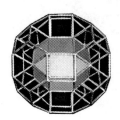

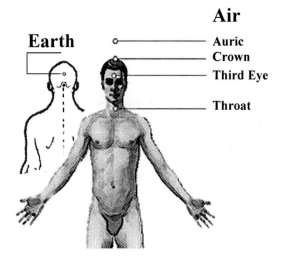

Test point for the circuits integrated by the
Embryonic Terra Prana Sphere and Gaia Terra Prana Sphere
in The 13th Circuit Ceremony

Embryonic Terra Prana
Sphere

Gaia Terra Prana
Sphere

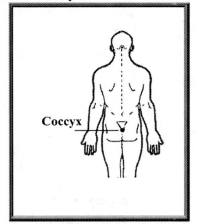

Integrates

AQUA SPHERE /
ICONIC AQUA SPHERE

WATER

**This 8th form in The 13th Circuit Ceremony
is a combination of:**

Aqua Sphere

Iconic Aqua Sphere

**The circuits of the Foundation Ceremony activated and integrated
by the Aqua Sphere and Iconic Aqua Sphere**

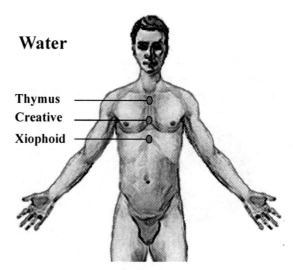

Water

Thymus
Creative
Xiophoid

**This combination of male and female
geometries activates and integrates
the Water circuits.**

**Test points for the circuits activated and integrated
by the Aqua Sphere and Iconic Aqua Sphere
in The 13th Circuit Ceremony**

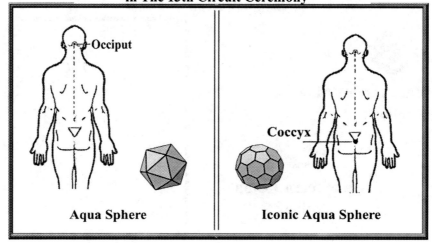

Occiput

Coccyx

Aqua Sphere

Iconic Aqua Sphere

Activates

Integrates

SOLAR SPHERE / ICONIC SOLAR SPHERE

ETHER

This 9th form in The 13th Circuit Ceremony is a combination of:

Solar Sphere

Iconic Solar Sphere

The circuits of the Foundation Ceremony activated and integrated by the Solar Sphere and Iconic Solar Sphere

This combination of male and female geometries activates and integrates the Ether circuits.

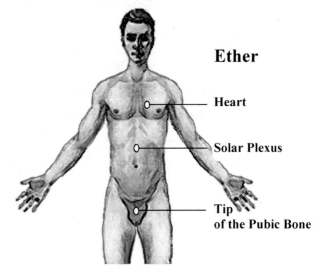

Ether

Heart

Solar Plexus

Tip of the Pubic Bone

Test points for the circuits activated and integrated by the Solar Sphere and Iconic Solar Sphere in The 13th Circuit Ceremony

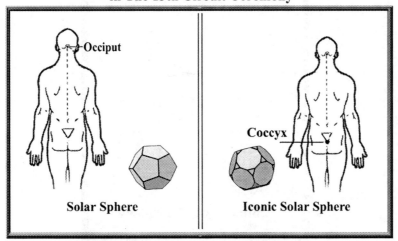

Occiput

Solar Sphere

Coccyx

Iconic Solar Sphere

Activates   **Integrates**

EMBRYONIC SOLAR SPHERE

ETHER

This 10th form in The 13th Circuit Ceremony is the:

Embryonic Solar Sphere

The circuits of the Foundation Ceremony integrated by the Embryonic Solar Sphere

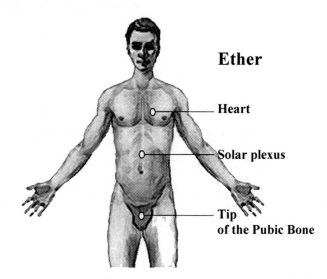

Ether

Heart

Solar plexus

Tip
of the Pubic Bone

This female geometric form integrates the Ether circuits.

Test point for the circuits integrated by the Embryonic Solar Sphere in The 13th Circuit Ceremony

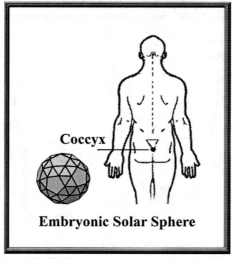

Coccyx

Embryonic Solar Sphere

Integrates

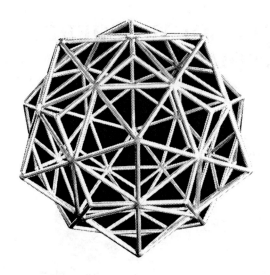

AQUA SOLAR SPHERE /
ICONIC AQUA SOLAR SPHERE

WATER and ETHER

**This 11th form in The 13th Circuit Ceremony
is a combination of:**

Aqua Solar Sphere

Iconic Aqua Solar Sphere

**The circuits of the Foundation Ceremony activated and integrated
by the Aqua Solar Sphere and Iconic Aqua Solar Sphere**

**This combination of male and female
geometries activates and integrates
the Water and Ether circuits.**

**The Aqua Solar Sphere
is the 3rd of the mirrored geometries.
In this case the Aqua and Solar Spheres
mirror each other. The Iconic Aqua Solar
Sphere is formed as the integrating lines
between the two.**

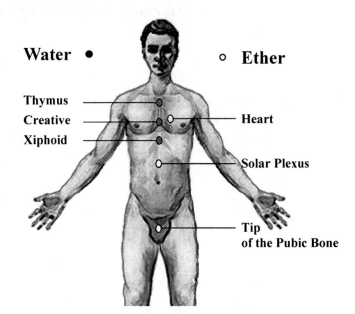

Water ● ○ Ether

Thymus
Creative
Xiphoid

Heart
Solar Plexus
Tip
of the Pubic Bone

**Test points for the circuits activated and integrated
by the Aqua Solar Sphere and Iconic Aqua Solar Sphere
in The 13th Circuit Ceremony**

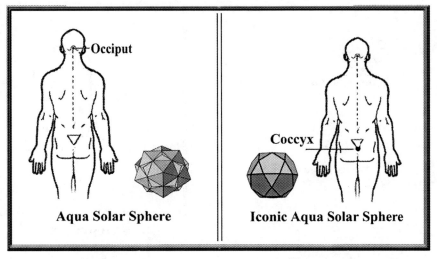

Occiput

Coccyx

Aqua Solar Sphere

Iconic Aqua Solar Sphere

Activates

Integrates

EMBRYONIC AQUA SOLAR SPHERE / GAIA AQUA SOLAR SPHERE

WATER and ETHER

This 12th form in The 13th Circuit Ceremony is a combination of:

Embryonic Aqua Solar Sphere

Gaia Aqua Solar Sphere

The circuits of the Foundation Ceremony integrated
by the Embryonic Aqua Solar Sphere and Gaia Aqua Solar Sphere

This combination of female
geometries integrates the
Water and Ether circuits.

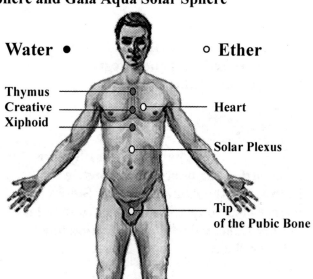

Water ●   ○ Ether

Thymus
Creative
Xiphoid

Heart

Solar Plexus

Tip
of the Pubic Bone

Test point for the circuits integrated
by the Embryonic Aqua Solar Sphere and Gaia Aqua Solar Sphere
in The 13th Circuit Ceremony

Embryonic Aqua Solar Sphere

Gaia Aqua Solar Sphere

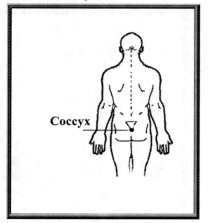

Coccyx

Integrates

MAHA SPHERE / GAIA SPHERE

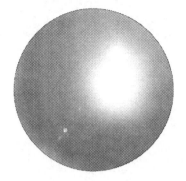

**This 13th form in The 13th Circuit Ceremony
is a Sphere**

As the most comprehensive form of consciousness
the Sphere contains all alchemical elements of creation.
It is the Monadic form of Divine Androgeny
and both activate and integrate the 13th Circuit.

Test points for the circuit activated and integrated
by the Maha Sphere and Gaia Sphere
in The 13th Circuit Ceremony

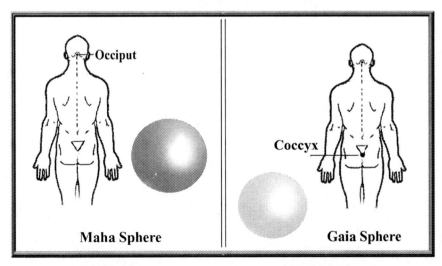

Activates   **Integrates**

Breath, the sacred unspoken vow between spirit and matter

The Sacred Breath Ceremony

As you weave your way through this euphoric Ceremony
that utilizes 14 stunning pieces of stellated Geometry,
unifying with the cosmic directive, embracing the Earth pulsations,
immersing yourself in the rhythmic tides of prana,
merging with the never ending One eternal breath that is shared
by every living thing, drifting beyond the reach of time,
you feel yourself a part of the spherical mandala
of the universal hologram as it unfolds and displays to you
its fractal composition in a starry array
that stirs remembrance...
awakening your quintessential identity...
starchild that you are...

... breath, the molecular cohesion that crystallizes spirit into form,
the unspoken vow between spirit and matter,
the cohesive divine influence that allows for the stimulation
of the cerebral cortex and the intricate brain chemistry
that gives the eyes the gift of sight,
the ears of sound, the heart to feel.

Breath is the bridge to consciousness,
the transformation of awareness into form and motion,
the medium through which we witness the daily miracle.

Breath - The Worldbridger

In the Soul Covenant, embedded within the Human matrix,
is a holonomic symbiotic code in which Human design
is the sensory organ for planetary ascension as Earth is the sensory
organ for Human ascension. The catalytic component that crystallizes
the alchemy of this divine union is light. Light is assimilated
through prana. Prana is assimilated through breath.
Through this co-creative interaction the hologram reveals itself,
as breath weaves the matrix into coherence.

Prana is the life-directive made accessible to the Human hologram
through molecular resonance. With each breath we step into
the wheel of eternal existence, sharing the One eternal breath
that is shared by every living thing on every planet, in every solar
system, in every galaxy of every universe.

Your breath escorts you into the churning mandalas of co-creative,
interactive fractals that compose the holographic template
of all manifest existence... you are not only you, you are the universe.
Each breath affects the whole because you are the whole.
You are the Source.
As the holographic emissaries of prime consciousness
you are fractals of the One...of the Monad.

The degree to which you are able to translate the pranic code
is the degree to which you integrate, synthesize and crystallize
the monadic prime consciousness within the Benevolent Heart
of Creation into your own Human template, becoming a conscious
conduit of light and love, stepping into your light body...
into the immortal continuum through your breath.

The Pranic Mechanism

Prana is drawn into the body from the heart center,
from the central fractal of the Human hologram.
Within the geometric Human matrix this is the stellated cube
octahedron or the Iconic Terra Prana Star - the stargate
through which the pranic creation code emanating from Source
infiltrates the body system to interface with the chakra systems.
As air is drawn into the body system from the atmosphere,
it is decoded by the chakra systems to alchemically catalyze
the pranic code. Breath is the synthesis of prana and air.
It is the combination of the conscious drawing in of prana,
the pranic circuitry, the chakra systems,
and the pranic causeway that encompasses the spinal column,
which, together, comprise the holonomic system
that is the pranic mechanism.

The more that circuitry connects into this mechanism, the more
the chakra systems are able to synthesize the molecular structure
of air with the pranic code and the more of this code
can be utilized within the pranic causeway.
(See Pranic Causeway)

169

The 6th Element - Stellar Radiance

*In the Ceremony of Sacred Breath, all of the Geometries used are
stellated, integrating as they do the 6th element of Stellar Radiance.
Stellar Radiance is that form of light that carries the creation code
of prana. Prana is the primal form of radiant intelligence before it is
translated into the differentiated spectrums of color that we know
as light. The light we see and translate, as emanating from our Sun,
is the Sun's translation of the prana code emanating from the
Heart of the Cosmos. As this radiance enters the heart of the solar
hologram it is translated and transmitted through the lensing system
of its own pranic mechanism and is transmitted as
the solar matrix of the immortal continuum in a form of light.
This translation of radiance becomes usable data for the
bio-computational field of the Human unit of circuitry to decode
and utilize, a code to activate and integrate the symbiosis
between the inhabitants of Earth and the solar system.
(see 'The Sun and Immortality')*

*Our Sun is the mediator of Galactic Intelligence projected
as radiant light from the Benevolent Source of Creation.
Each one of us is a star projecting the Human form of pranic
intelligence particular to planet Earth.*

*It is the presence of these geometric formulae of radiant light
that activates and integrates the resonant stellar code
within the Soul Covenant.*

*In the Ceremony of Sacred Breath, it is the 2 Stars of Immortality,
the Gaia Terra Prana Star and the Gaia Aqua Solar Star,
which reconnect the Roof of the Mouth and the Fontanelle circuits.
The pranic mechanism is activated and integrated,
together with the Lung, Penis/Clitoris, Testes/Ovaries,
Sacrum and Umbilical circuits (through the stimulation of accelerated
electromagnetic input), to decode a wider spectrum of the pranic code.*

The full pranic code holds the immortal harmonic.
Once the Human bio-computational unit of circuitry
is fully connected into the creation mechanism of the universal
holography, it is then able to decode the full spectrum
of the intelligence data present in prana.
The immortal harmonic synthesizes and crystallizes
with the incarnate body presence, unifying the physical matrix
with the design pattern of the original blueprint present
in the Geometric Soul Covenant... resurrecting the light-body.

In the Ceremony of Sacred Breath, the activation and integration
of the pranic mechanism is initiated through the reconnection
of 7 circuits into this system. It is the circuitry
of the 'Temple of Time Ceremony' that reconnects
the pranic mechanism into the space/time continuum
of solar/galactic holography.

The 'One Circuit' of The Ceremony of Universal Unification,
which awakens the universal symbiosis that exists between
the Human entity and the Benevolent Heart of Creation,
allows for the decoding of the full pranic transmission
that is the Breath of Immortality.

Breathing Through the Heart

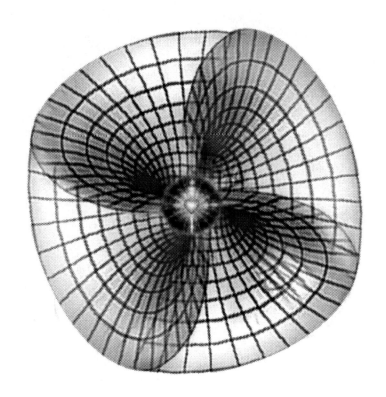

The Breath of Immortality
Becoming Breath

*Due to the atrophy of the endocrine system and the disconnection
of circuitry into the pranic mechanism, we engage in shallow,
unconscious breathing, absorbing enough of the catalytic agent
of oxygen to decode just enough pranic nourishment to maintain
the virtual semblance of our genetically modified, disconnected,
incarnate body presence - in this frequency zone.
Although it is undeniably beneficial to practice conscious breathing
techniques that will serve to energize the heart/mind/body system,
bringing more mental clarity, and even physical rejuvenation,
it is not until the entire pranic mechanism is functioning at optimum
drive, that the full code of pranic intelligence will be available
to the Human bio-computational system.
It is not until this occurs that the Human being will come into total
symbiotic resonance with the holography of cosmic consciousness
and activate the inherent schematic of conscious evolution that will
reconnect our race and planet, back into the cosmic embrace.*

*It was our belief, when we first began to hold The Ceremony
of Sacred Breath, that we could teach others to practice the Breath
of Immortality. However, it was not until we experienced the
reconnection of the 7 circuits of The Temple of Time Ceremony that
we realized that our perceptions of breath and prana were dualistic.
Instead of the Breath of Immortality circulating (as we had imagined)
through the body, it is in fact a process of holographic infusion,
a movement that has no beginning and no end.*

Conscious breathing was not a discipline, but a way of being.

*Here I will attempt to translate this holonomic function to the nearest
fractal of my comprehension!*

*It will be far easier to follow and exercise this breath meditation
after the reconnection of the 7 Pranic circuits in The Sacred Breath
Ceremony, and even more so after The Temple of Time Ceremony.
This 'way-of-being breath' will be practiced in the workshop
and will become more comprehensible in the experience of it.*

Becoming Breath Meditation

The opalescent radiant field of the pranic mechanism
that encases your presence is a torus of active energy.

There is no beginning, there is no end, to this energy field.

However, because you are coming from this dimension of perception,
you need to 'begin' somewhere!

Begin in your heart.

Receive Breath

Drawing prana from the 'infinite in' of your Heart center, you will
automatically find that you are drawing air in from the 'infinite out'.
Become aware that these two sacred substances are experiencing
an alchemical cohesion within the many chambers and systems
of the alchemic crucible that is your body-temple, creating through
the sacred vow between spirit and matter, the magical,
alchemical nourishment that gives your eyes the gift of sight,
your ears to hear, your heart to feel...
each breath is the bridge to the daily miracle of life.

Each breath brings consciousness.

Give Breath

Filling your body and auric field with breath, offer back your life,
your love to the Source, expelling your pranic breath from your
Heart center through the Throat, Third Eye, Crown, Auric, Solar,
Galactic and Universal chakras - drawing this breath from
the Source within you to the Source within the heart
of the universal holography of Creation.

Receive Breath

*Draw this prana back from Source, through these upper chakras
into the Heart center. As Source feeds every infinitesimal point
in the unified field, breath is accepted from everything.
Your body is filled with Source energy flowing through everything
that appears to be on the outside of you. As you pull this into your
heart, realize that it is drawn back through the heart gate from the
infinite in, once again filling the heart, the body, the auric field.*

Give Breath

*Visualize the breath passing the Heart/Source center through the
Solar, Procreation, Survival, Earth and Crystalline Core chakras…
offering your life, your love, to the Heart of Gaia.*

Receive Breath

Receive your breath back through the lower chakras into the heart.

*This pattern of giving and receiving 'life/love/breath' creates and is
a torus. The heart is at the center, as a holographic hyper-infinity
figure-of-eight that embraces the Human energy field.
Speed up this process so that this flow happens many times in each
movement of breath, ultimately merging the 'receive breath' with
the 'give breath', simultaneously offering and receiving, exchanging
prana, life force, energy, love, with Gaia and Galactic Center,
realizing your place in the flow of Stellar Radiance,
as it passes through you traveling from and to
every reference point in the unified field,*

the One Breath shared by every living being.

Chakras

"The mind is more powerful than any particle accelerator, more sensitive that any radio receiver or the largest optical telescope, more complete in its grasp of information than any computer. The human body - its voice, its power of locomotion and its imagination - is a more than sufficient means for the exploration of any time or energy level in the universe."   Terence McKenna

*The mycelium of visible and invisible energy systems that co-create the holography of the Human heart/body/mind system is of a complexity and intricacy that defies explanation in isolation or in terms of linear thinking and dualistic language; none more so than the chakra system.
This book, and The Template model as a whole, is primarily focused upon the circuitry system as this is the most primal delivery system of the electromagnetic creation directive emanating from the heart of the universal hologram.
This is the system that is reinstated via the Ceremony codes.*

In the Chinese tradition, 3,000 meridians (circuits) are cited as part of the Human energy system. In the 7th century Upanishads of the Hindu tradition 72,000 meridians are involved in the flow of vital force within the heart system alone. In The Template model, due to the complexity of this system, it has been distilled into a skeletal structure of major circuitry.

*A similar situation exists within the chakra system.
Many ancient and modern traditions seek to explain and describe the progression of chakras in the body, allotting to each one color, element, sound, bodily function, plane of existence, animal, sense organ, emotion, particular deity and so on. Some doctrines postulate the existence of 7 major chakras, some 13.
Others expound the significance of sub-chakras, of which the Third Eye has 7.*

The classic illustrations of the basic chakra systems that traditionally form a vertical column up the center of the body were ostensibly created as focal points for meditation - iconographic symbols arranged in such a way for the linear mind to classify, organize, and comprehend.

Throughout history to the present time various associations
and classifications have been projected upon these centers.
These projections have been colored by cultural
and religious belief systems.

It is the aim of The Template model to honor all of this incredible
intuited knowledge as many facets of the same jewel.
However, for our purposes, we will distil the system to a simple basic
form and focus primarily on the function of the chakras as a whole
and holonomic system of energy translation.
We also recognize that our understanding of their construct
and function is in a state of flux as we realize the chakra system
to be a field of multi-dimensional interfaces.

The chakras are holographic, inter-dimensional portals that link
the body system from one dimension of expression to another.
Each chakra is hyper-elemental and opalescent in its churning
rainbow hues of never-still light reflecting labyrinths of multilevel
energy-transforming components. These dataflow translators
are the interface between the circuitry delivery system and the ability
of the computational unit of circuitry to translate and transmit
this blueprint code into the incarnate body presence - portals
of translation between the iconic patterning of the life-directive
and the conceptual reality of manifestation within every living entity.

As such the chakra system is evolving: the more that the
electromagnetic dataflow is accelerated via the reconnection
of circuitry, the more of the Soul Covenant is tangibly embodied -
a fuller spectrum of the chakra system is resurrected to deal with
the task of translating the creation code as usable data for the
endocrine system and its bio-informational signaling system.

In the following chapter on the geometry and circuits
of The Sacred Breath Ceremony, the chakra system is referred to
in general terms as we have suspended at this time any tendency
to compartmentalize this complicated system in our anticipation
of a more holistic future understanding.

Breath
is the bridge to consciousness,
the transformation
of awareness
into form and motion,
the medium through which
we witness
the daily miracle

The Stars
of
The Sacred Breath
Ceremony

Solar Stargate
The Portal to the Immortal

*The first chakra to decode prana is at the roof of the mouth
and is activated by taking breath in through the nose. This triggers
the resonant pranic receptors in the cerebral cortex to awaken
the pranic mechanism. The entire chakra system
is a part of the pranic mechanism.*

*As we enter The Sacred Breath Ceremony the stargate into
this stunning 14 star Ceremony is opened with the Solar Star.
This star is the only stellated Platonic solid in the Ceremony.
The Solar Star is an interlacing of pentagrams.
It is reminiscent of Celtic knot work, never ending or beginning,
and represents the unborn, never dying, eternal and everlasting
nature of the immortal paradigm. The frequency of this star
echoes the joy of sentient sovereign existence and is resonant
with that part of the Soul Covenant that represents the Tree of Life.
It is the foundation of the Ether/Solar code that unifies
with the Water/Aqua code to integrate, synthesize and crystallize
into the Gaia Aqua Star. The Tree of Life is a fractal frequency
of the immortal harmonic.*

*In the Stargate Ceremony the Third Eye chakra system
is integrated with the Heart center.
The Lung circuit is reconnected.*

Solar Stargate

Solar Star

Solar Sphere

**This Star is created
by stellating the Solar Sphere.**

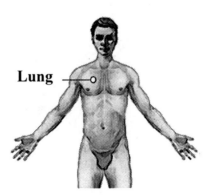

Lung ——o

**The test point for the circuit connected by the
Solar Star
is over the Lung.**

The Ceremony of Integration

*In the Ceremony of Integration, the Geometric Alchemy takes
the form of 5 autonomous Iconic Spheres of Fire, Earth, Air, Water
and Ether integrated with the 6th element of Stellar Radiance.
The Iconic model within the Soul Covenant that defines
the quintessence of the Human identity as a sensate earthly
manifestation of the Galactic Directive, linked
in to the eternal continuum, is integrated electromagnetically.
A resonant octave of the harmonic of the Tree of Knowledge
is awakened and reactivated through 2 circuits within the pranic
mechanism; the Penis/Clitoris and the Testicles/Ovaries.
The Perineum and Coccyx chakra systems are
integrated with the Heart center.*

Integrating Geometry

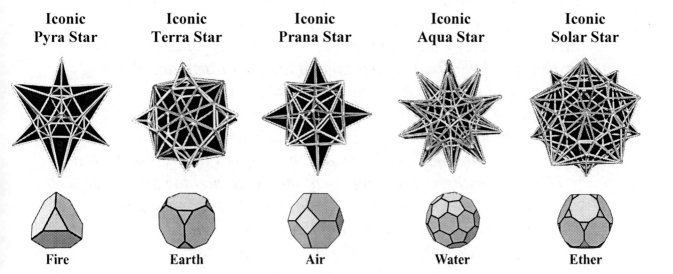

Iconic Pyra Star	Iconic Terra Star	Iconic Prana Star	Iconic Aqua Star	Iconic Solar Star
Fire	Earth	Air	Water	Ether

These stars are created by stellating the five elemental Iconic Gaia Spheres

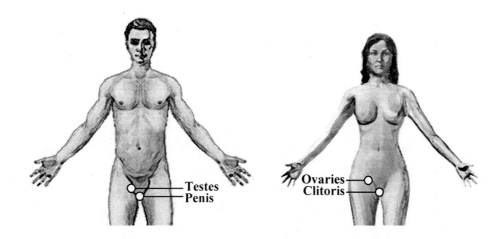

**The test points for the circuits connected
by these 5 stars are the
Testes/Penis and Ovaries/Clitoris.**

The Ceremony of Synthesis

In the Ceremony of Synthesis, the components of Geometric Alchemy
take the form of two autonomous Embryonic Spheres unified
with the 6th element of Stellar Radiance to form the Embryonic
Terra Star and the Embryonic Solar Star.
It is in this Ceremony that the matrix of form is recognized as being
constructed of the Tantric language of light, as Earth and Ether
are reunited within the arena of the psyche.
This is a part of the 'archetypal cleanse' in which Heaven and Earth
are synthesized and recognized as one and the same.
The harmonic within the Soul Covenant that defines the quintessential
Human identity as the progeny of the Earth and the Sun,
is awakened electromagnetically through the reconnection
of the Umbilical circuit within the pranic mechanism.
The Earth, Throat and Auric chakra systems
are integrated with the Heart center.

Synthesis Geometry

Embryonic Terra Star   **Embryonic Solar Star**

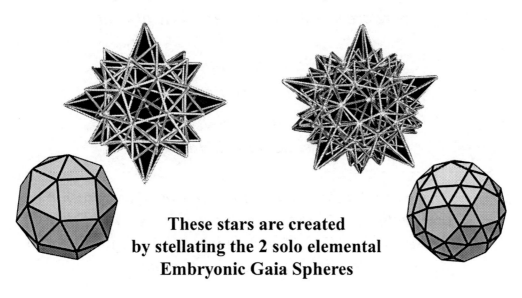

These stars are created
by stellating the 2 solo elemental
Embryonic Gaia Spheres

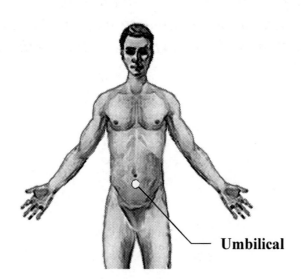

—— Umbilical

The test point for the circuit connected
by these 2 stars is just below the navel.

The Ceremony of Unity

*In the Ceremony of Unity, we come to the heart of The Sacred
Breath Ceremony, to the heart of the Soul Covenant,
to the Heart of the Cosmos.*

There are 4 stars in the Ceremony of Unity:

Iconic Terra Prana Star
Embryonic Terra Prana Star
Iconic Aqua Solar Star
Embryonic Aqua Solar Star

*These are the stellated configurations of integration
and synthesis of Earth and Air, and Water and Ether.
It is these combinations that accelerate into Crystallization
in the final stage of this Ceremony.*

*The presence of these combinations within the code
ensures the reconnection of the Sacral circuit
within the living crucible of birth - the sacrum.*

Unity Geometry

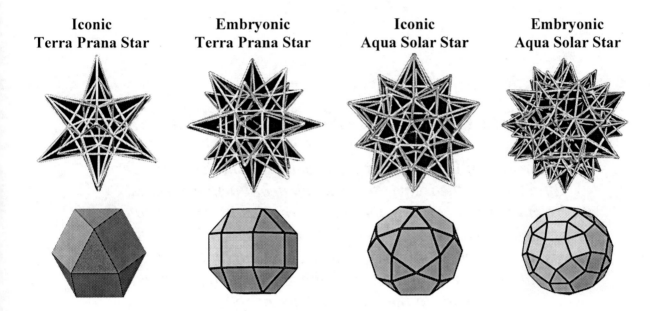

Iconic Terra Prana Star
Embryonic Terra Prana Star
Iconic Aqua Solar Star
Embryonic Aqua Solar Star

**These stars are created by stellating the
Iconic Terra Prana, Embryonic Terra Prana, Iconic Aqua Solar
and Embryonic Aqua Solar Spheres**

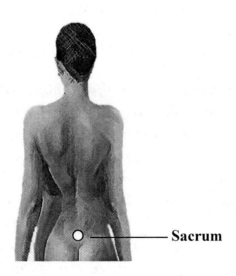

Sacrum

**The test point for the circuit connected
by these 4 stars is the Sacrum.**

The Heart Star - Soul of the Soul

*The Ceremony of Unity begins spectacularly with the Iconic Terra
Prana Star...the Heart Star. The 'clay' of Earth embraces
the breath of life, accepting the Human race as its prime mediator
of intelligence projected as light from her star lover, the Sun
- as was agreed within the original Covenant that was sealed
with the symbol of the Bird Tribe, the ancient promise
given to the Earth and her people.*

**Every diversion from the living truth of nature,
every lie we have told, every heart broken, every drop of blood
spilt in battle, every motherless child is born of this disconnection.
These wounds of the cosmic orphan, lost in unnatural
time/space co-ordinates, are not born of shame or guilt.
There is no 'original sin', no 'fall from grace'.
The boundless omnipotent Heart of Creation is unconditional.**

*The central fractal within the Human holonomic mechanism
is the Iconic Terra Prana Star...the Heart Star. It is through this
junction that all systems within the interactive, interconnecting
mechanism of the Human matrix are interwoven. It is the fulcrum point
through which we embody the Benevolence of Creation.
Within the individual unified field of each Human entity,
it is the very soul of the soul.
The heart, as it is now universally understood, has always been
pinpointed as the seat of 'love', as the center from which compassion,
understanding and forgiveness emanate. This is because
the heart center is the central fractal of the Human hologram
from which emanates the "One Circuit" that unifies all life forms
with the Benevolent Source of Creation.*

It is through this center that we are able to allow the purest form
of this benevolence and, to the extent of our ability, express it Humanly.
It is not that the heart chakra center is in someway more spiritual
or more important, it is its positioning within the whole system
that makes it an energetic terminus for the inflow of Source data
and the outflow of cognizant feedback.

"I am the sensory expression of the Benevolence of Creation"

This is the mantra for the Heart Star. It is a sonic frequency that,
when unified with the manifest form of the Iconic Terra Prana Star
(Heart Star), 'opens' the heart center and stimulates the production
of endorphins. Endorphins are a sacred salve which eradicates fear
through the re-instigation of divine identity. The entire Sacred Breath
Ceremony stimulates the production of this hormone through
the acceleration of pranic nourishment (prana being
the dataflow from the Benevolence of Creation).

The Heart Star, as it is placed within the Soul Covenant,
is in frequency resonance with the heart chakra.
When this center is performing at its optimum ability, it acts
as the ultimate decoding transmitter, able to synthesize and transmute
all incoming data from the entire chakra system. The frequency
with which this chakra center is able to spin dictates the resonance
between the manifest physical Human form and its light-body.

The light-body exists at a hyper-spin frequency in resonance with
the Omnipotent Heart of Creation - the higher the spin frequency
of the Human heart center, the greater the resonance with
the light-body and the ability to unify with it. When these bodies
come into total alignment, the transformation from carbon base
to crystalline is complete... true actualization
of transubstantiation... transcendence.

The frequency of this center's spin is reliant upon the density
of 'conditions' laid upon its function. The vibration of fear
as a result of the conditions of abandonment and betrayal
greatly subdue the spin frequency. As a result of the modification
of the Human DNA and the disconnection of circuitry,
the part of the Covenant which maintains connection to Source

and coherent comprehension of quintessential identity has become
deactivated, materializing within the 'heart' of Humanity
a deep condition of abandonment and betrayal. This condition
is played out endlessly in a myriad of diverse dramas
that plague, to some degree, all relationships.

On a global scale, this disconnection has materialized as a massive
paranoia and has galvanized a fragmentation of self-realization (born
of an erroneous definition of God) as religion tears the world apart.

The healing of abandonment and betrayal is initiated by the return
of resonance within the Heart Star and the reactivation of the part
of the Soul Covenant that defines the Human as an aspect
of its Source and, thus, an emissary of that Source's potential
as a creator of life. Through this embrace of core identity
is born the true definition of our sexuality. It is this - the most
powerful and self-regenerative Human ability - that defines us
as the universal progenitors of life and the harbingers
of the Light Family...the Bird Tribe.
In the true fecundity of our sexual identity is our liberation.

It is in the Ceremony of Unity, of which the Heart Star is an alchemical
component, that Sacred Breath integrates and synthesizes the Earth,
Perineum, Coccyx, and Third Eye chakra systems
through the Heart chakra/center.

This is the seed breath that germinates into the Breath of Immortality.
Once the pathway is cleared between these 5 centers,
the Breath of Immortality activates and integrates
the light-body matrix in preparation for the actualization
of the transcendental Human form...the "Resurrection".

In the Ceremony of Unity, the Heart Star is followed by the Embryonic
Terra Prana Star. In this Embryonic stage the Iconic quintessential
Human identity, introduced by the Heart Star, is synthesized
into the body presence.
It is this star that morphs (in the Ceremony of Crystallization)
into one of the 2 Stars of Immortality - the Gaia Terra Prana Star -
crystallizing the divine Human potential and unifying the polarized
gender expression to form the Divine Androgyne.
(See Stars of Immortality).

Iconic Aqua Solar Star and Embryonic Aqua Solar Star

*On planet Earth, water is the most easily imbued element
and is perfectly constructed to embrace the subtleties of meaning
carried in the Ether code. The merging of water and light
produces a stunning display of elements. Consider the diamond-like
explosions of fractal beams of radiance that occur when the Sun
is caught dancing on the ocean waves near sunset!*

*In the Foundation Ceremony, the subtleties of the Ether code
are introduced into the Human electromagnetic field as energetic
information through the reconnection of the Ether circuits:
Solar (solar plexus), Heart and Pubic. In the 1st Ceremony,
the sonic resonant code employed to resurrect these Ether circuits
acknowledges the original Human as a Servant Warrior of the Sun,
a member of the Bird Tribe, descended into Human form
from the mind of light beyond the Sun, whose quintessential function
is as a biological unit of circuitry translating the solar
information matrix into the unified field of earthly manifestation.*

***It is in discovering the co-creative nature
of our relationship with the Sun and the Earth
that our quintessential identity is revealed to us.
For we are children playing between Earth and stars ...
it is through us that the heart of our Mother is illuminated.***

*In the 1st Ceremony, the reconnection of the Water circuits begins
the stabilization of the emotional infrastructure of the physical
Human identity. This takes the participants back before
the first breath is taken, back to the soul decision before conception,
not only to take full responsibility for their lives but also to reconnect
with the depth of their gratitude for such an honor.
This puts in place a strong and stable platform on which to prepare
the emotional body to align with the spiritual identity.*

*In the Ceremony of Unity, the 2 elements of Water and Ether unify
and join with the 6th element of Stellar Radiance. This forms
the stellated geometric formula that integrates and synthesizes
the fractal of the Soul Covenant that contracts our ability to act,
via the Sun, as electromagnetic mediators between Earth
and the Galactic Core, through the reconnection of the Sacral circuit.
This renders the alembic crucible of the sacrum
a 'Chalice of Life Eternal'.*

The Ceremony of Crystallization

The Stars of Immortality
Gaia Terra Prana Star and Gaia Aqua Solar Star

*All the geometric fractals of the Soul Covenant employed
in The Template Ceremonies hold the immortal harmonic.
However, in the 2 crystalline Gaia Stars, the 3 phases
of manifestation come together in 1 geometric data storage unit;
forming a complete harmonic of the Tree of Knowledge
and the Tree of Life. These 2 geometric configurations mirror
that part of the Soul Covenant that bridges the dimensions.*

*The presence of these configurations in the Ceremony
of Crystallization integrates the entire chakra system beginning
in the Crystalline Core through the Earth, Survival, Procreation,
Solar Plexus, Heart, Throat, Third Eye, Crown, Auric, Solar
and Galactic chakras to then circle back to the Crystalline Core.*

*This charts not only the map of the integrating system
of chakra centers but also the 'Circuit of Breath' that charts
the Breath of Immortality to include the Galactic Core
(the 'One Circuit' that connects this circuit to the Universal circuit
is reconnected in the 6th Ceremony). This circle of breath
is the 7th circuit of the pranic mechanism and connects
the Human unit of circuitry through the Roof of the Mouth
and Fontanelle circuits.*

*In the Ceremony of Crystallization, the Tree of Knowledge
and the Tree of Life are united to share spatial cognizance
through the same circuit.*

Crystallization Geometry

Gaia Terra Prana Star   **Gaia Aqua Solar Star**

These stars are created by stellating
—— the Gaia Terra Prana and
Gaia Aqua Solar Spheres ——

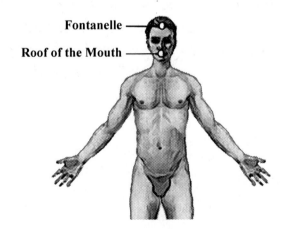

Fontanelle ——

Roof of the Mouth ——

The test points for the circuits connected
by the Crystallization Stars are the
Fontanelle and the Roof of the Mouth.

Gaia Terra Prana Star

The Gaia Terra Prana Star is positioned in the Soul Covenant
as both the source and the reality of the Tree of Knowledge.
The Tree of Knowledge is that part of the immortal aspect
of the Covenant that defines the Human as the full expression
of Divine Androgyny. It holds the full spectrum potential
of the emancipated Human procreative ability -
the ability to procreate outside of the birth/life/death cycle
that is a part of the present dualistic paradigm.
It is through the realization of this emancipated sexual identity
that the unborn, eternal race will come into being.

Gaia Aqua Solar Star

The Gaia Aqua Solar Star is positioned in the Soul Covenant
as both the source and the reality of the Tree of Life.
The Tree of Life is that part of the immortal aspect of the Covenant
that defines the Human as a sovereign sentient instrument
for the Benevolence of Creation functioning as
a conscious conduit of life eternal.

The Sacred Day Ceremony
Ceremonial attunement to the living truth

Do you have an altar in your home?

*An altar in the home provides a cohesive central focus for all
that you wish to create in your reality. It is symbolic of your path
and holds upon it the components of your personal alchemy,
your integrated physical/spiritual signature. It reveals that which you
hold most dear and relevant to your conscious evolution.
Without an altar your home is a series of compartments
in which to survive, find shelter and keep your belongings!*

*The absence of an altar in the home is a sign of our western culture's
overemphasis on material existence and the surrender
of the autonomous spiritual search into the hands
of the professional mediators of orthodox religion.
An altar turns the home into a temple,
a place of healing and transformation.*

Sacred Space

*Give your altar its own space rather than sticking it on the end of the
mantelpiece or desktop! Position it centrally rather than peripherally.*

*Having an altar will spontaneously draw you into meditation.
It is the most central and ancient form of Feng Shui.
It is a statement that your path is as you make it.*

*You will find that the components on your altar will require change
as you change. They will also attract and hold energies that
require cleansing, and it is advisable to maintain your altar daily;
you will find that as you do so you will be keeping the integration
and synthesis of change and transmutation flowing within
your own spiritual evolution, making it more conscious.*

*As your altar forms the nucleus of daily existence you
will find yourself far more organized on a domestic level.*

Your altar magically holds and stabilizes your most fundamental manifest infrastructure on which to build the integrity of your life, subconsciously providing you with behavioral reference points that reflect your highest purpose as you navigate the chaos of the everyday world.

Be clear as to what you put on your altar. Whatever it is it will subliminally affect your subconscious. On close inspection, you may find objects and symbology that hold your consciousness in outmoded, patriarchal and inappropriate religious patterns, objects that you are holding onto for sentimental value that in fact 'dis-empower'.
If you are in doubt, simple muscle testing can help. (Having cleared the denial point with the pulse synchronization meditation, look at the object and have someone test your strength).

We find, even as we endlessly travel, that in the most grim motorway motel, the first thing we do is put out a few aesthetic objects that can constitute an altar. This continually defines our priorities, grounding our awareness, preventing us from being drawn into the prevailing frequency of global insanity.

In order to practice the Sacred Day Ceremony it is advisable to have on your altar manifest representatives of the 6 elements. Any stellated piece of geometry will represent the 6th element of Stellar Radiance, and the Creation Mandala (Flower of Life) represents the all-encompassing configuration of Source.

Manifest Elements

Water	*decorative bowl of water. If desired place in it a floating flower or crystal.*
Air	*incense.*
Earth	*crystal or stone.*
Fire	*candle.*
Ether	*internal visualization of the Sun or the Platonic or Archimedean solid of Ether: (Solar Sphere (dodecahedron) or Solar Star).*
Stellar Radiance	*any form of geometric star. A star tetrahedron can be constructed out of card.*
Creation Mandala	*Flower of Life, can be drawn.*

It is generally a good idea to dress your altar with fresh flowers daily - this is symbolic of vigilance and commitment whilst also adding an element of celebration. Infusing color, sound and scent with each Ceremonial occasion creates a sense of enjoyment and celebration rather than a discipline.

Begin with the "Breath of Fire".

For those who have not experienced The Ceremony of Sacred Breath or have forgotten this breathing modality:

Assume a full star position: arms held away from the body, feet apart, using the abdominal muscles to draw and expel breath rapidly in and out of the lungs.
This form of breathing draws the kundalini up from the coccyx and harmonizes this rejuvenating sexual/creative energy with the Heart and Third Eye chakras.
This infusion of prana through conscious breathing enhances the function of Ceremony to stimulate the cerebral cortex and create ultra-receptive brain chemistry.

In The Sacred Day Ceremony you are establishing a stimulus/response pattern based on the alchemical components of the creative force... the elements.

This establishes the natural world as the infrastructure of your behavioral reference: the natural world being the living body of truth. This pattern is being established through the engagement of the senses: vision, smell (immensely evocative), touch (feel the water...touch it to your Third Eye ... the warmth of the flame, the vibration of the crystal, evoke the feeling of the Sun's warmth on your face) and sonic resonance through the linguistic vibration of the spoken word.

It's Elemental

Elements are the building blocks of all manifest creation: as such they compose the most fundamental archetypal platform within the psyche. By redefining/re-establishing this archetypal strata, through the conscious communion of Ceremony, in which the sonic resonance of your Soul's Covenant provides an alchemical component, what you know indeed becomes who you are.

*The Sacred Day Ceremony also holds the essential patterning
of the codes that reconnected your circuitry and provides
a daily structure through which the physical, emotional and mental
bodies can integrate and synthesize the fertile transformational data
offered by circuitry reconnection. It also provides,
on a domestic daily level, in this time of global darkness,
a reminder of your quintessential identity
as conscious conduits of light and love.*

*The **Water** Ceremony can be silently said as you partake of water
either when bathing or drinking etc...*

*The **Air** Ceremony to return to conscious breathing.*

*The **Earth** Ceremony when you find yourself off center.*

*The **Fire** Ceremony as you light a candle.*

*The exquisite, powerful **Ether** Ceremony can be done at sunrise
or sunset to align with solar power and the geometric seed code
transmitted through the Sun's light. It is also an honoring
of this grand star as the giver of life. The Breath of Fire before
and after this Ceremony is exceptionally rejuvenating.*

*The **Stellar Radiance** Ceremony to release fear.*

*The **Creation Mandala** Ceremony to align with light.*

*You will soon know all these by heart, finding your own ways
to bring them into your lives. As you move through each element,
spend a few moments on the miraculous presence of that element
in your life and what it means to you personally.
For instance with water: see it as the oceans, seas and rivers.
See it coursing through the veins of every leaf and blade of grass
as well as your own body. See it as rain...as liquid crystal.
You may want to pick a particular element daily to hold
in the back of your mind: consciously and subconsciously
recognizing its presence as you move through your day.
Create an elemental talisman to wear, anchoring you
in your meditation, helping you to stay centered.*

*There are also videos, manuals and tapes in the making,
all as parts of a structure that we are putting together to assist
the Ceremonial initiate to stay actively connected with
The Template mission...to live ceremoniously.*

As you move through the Sacred Day Ceremony
know that there are many who do it with you,
in the UK, USA, Australia, New Zealand, South Africa, Guatemala,
Mexico, Bali, Egypt, Spain, Greece, Italy, Germany,
Sweden and France, a list that is growing.

Take a moment to feel your connection with them.

Visualize this connection as a laser grid of light energy.
As you breathe, you breathe together.

Each breath pulsates through this light consciousness grid
connecting you together in the One eternal breath
that is shared by every living thing;

on every planet,

in every solar system,

in every galaxy,

in every universe.

As our numbers grow, this grid will stabilize and form
a resonant global field of awareness, a love-based frequency,
a worldwide web of new consciousness.

This unified field, when it reaches critical mass, will provide
an archetypal behavioral reference for our brothers and sisters
across the globe to join spontaneously through resonance...

should they choose on a soul level to do so.

Make a difference

Each day is sacred

Ceremony is a seed...plant it

Sacred Day Ceremony

Water

This Sacred Day

My communion with the element of Water
Honors my physical being as a chalice
Overflowing with the purity of innocence

Understanding brings forgiveness
Cleansing my emotional body

My mental body releases judgment
As I recognize the perfection in all creation

Love is my protection

Air

This Sacred Day

My communion with the element of Air
Honors my physical being as infused by each breath
With the Benevolence of Creation

Compassion empowers my sense of self
Cleansing my emotional body

My mental body releases notions of separation
As breath integrates my sense of self into
the wheel of eternal existence

Love is my protection

Earth

This Sacred Day

My communion with the element of Earth
Honors my physical being as fully present
Upon this sentient planet

I honor my sensory self as connected to all creation
Cleansing my emotional body

My mental body releases fear
As I celebrate this incarnation,
strengthening my trust in each moment

Love is my protection

Fire

This Sacred Day

My communion with the element of Fire
Honors my physical being as eternal

I honor my connectedness
to the universal reservoir of pleasure and causal desire
Cleansing my emotional body

My mental body releases fear of death
As I recognize the illusion of duality

Love is my protection

Ether

This Sacred Day

My communion with the element of Ether
Honors my physical being as a child of the Earth and the Sun

Every ray of light defines my understanding of abundance
Cleansing my emotional body

My mental body releases the fear that is attachment
As I come to know there is no separation

Love is my protection

Stellar Radiance

This Sacred Day

My communion with the element of Stellar Radiance
Honors my physical being as assimilating
The rejuvenating power of the Tantric language of light

My every breath unites my physical being
with the Source of Creation
Cleansing my emotional body

My mental body releases fear
As with each breath I know myself
as sentient, sovereign, eternal

Love is my protection

Creation Mandala

This Sacred Day

This Ceremony of celebration
of the living word
Brings understanding of Source
Opening to me
Within me
I am the light
I hold the light
The light is with me always

Through my conscious communion
With the alchemical elements of creation
My spiritual identity merges in perfect union
With all other aspects of myself

This alchemy aligns
My Human expression
With my Soul's Covenant
To give and receive love
In all that I do
This Sacred Day

This I do for myself
and for all Humanity

The Seeding

The most vital aspect of The Template lies in the Codes.
Beyond the accumulation of information, The Template
gifts the initiate with Sacred Ceremonial formulae that trigger
the reconnection of the most fundamental life-force energy system,
to resurrect the masterpiece of the original Human design.

Your heart/body/mind system is your personal instrument
with which to function as an ambassador of light, an emissary of love,
a conduit through which the Benevolence of Creation can infuse
this reality, not only for your sake, but for the sake of those who,
in countries across the globe, can feel the shift in the quality of time
and light and know that portals of opportunity are opening
through which they can transcend the pain and suffering
that being Human has come to mean to them.

In the reconnection of your circuitry, you instigate an acceleration
of electromagnetic Source Consciousness into this time/space
frequency zone, undermining the present fear-based, conflict-riddled
predominant world structure simply by being; each one of you
adding a fractal of consciousness to the required critical mass
of the new paradigm hologram. This ultimately creates a stable
resonant field of evolutionary opportunity with which those
who are unable consciously to take part ceremoniously
can simply decide, on a soul level, to attune their being.

Your recalibrated vibration will be felt, by the tribal child
on the African plain whose mother has been taken by Aids,
by the pubescent soldier conscripted into a war he doesn't understand,
by the urban teenager reaching for his inherent right
to experience bliss by taking up a needle.

Remember, it is not so much about time as about numbers:
tell a friend!

The new paradigm will not be born of the mind alone.
The new paradigm will be understood in the mind,
felt in the heart and made tangible in the body.

Getting Connected

*For more information,
or to enquire about Ceremonies,
see our websites for Ambassadors
and Administration Centers.*

www.originalinnocence.com
www.thetemplate.org

Ceremony is a seed...plant it

Lightning Source UK Ltd.
Milton Keynes UK
UKOW01f1220130115

244409UK00004B/71/P